Variation in
British Butterflies

A. D. A. Russwurm, New Forest, June 1971

Variation in British Butterflies

by A. S. Harmer

Illustrated by A. D. A. Russwurm

84 specially commissioned plates of watercolours
by A. D. A. Russwurm

A. D. A. Russwurm's biography

53 colour photographs

12 black and white photographs and figures

8 diagrams

The Author and the Artist.
Alec Harmer and Donald Russwurm check over the first proofs of the paintings. Brockenhurst, April 1999.

To Maggie

For being so patient and understanding,
this book is lovingly dedicated.

First published in Great Britain in 2000 by 🦋 Paphia Publishing Ltd., Covertside, Sway Road, Lymington, Hampshire so41 8NN.

British Library Cataloguing-in-Publication Data.
A catalogue record for this book is available from the British Library.

ISBN 0 9537236 0 7

Designed and printed by Printwise of Lymington.

CONTENTS

FOREWORD

by T. G. Howarth, B.E.M., F.R.E.S.
(Formerly Senior Scientific Officer in the Department of Entomology,
Rhopalocera, British Museum Natural History. Retired 1976).

I have often been asked by lepidopterists, particularly those from abroad, why it is that aberrations hold such a fascination for the British butterfly collector. There seems to be no doubt that this is due to the paucity of our native species compared with those of the European continent and elsewhere.

Our knowledge concerning the variation of our Rhopalocera has increased remarkably during this century as a result of the continued and intensive field-work undertaken by enthusiasts (mainly amateur), through selective breeding, and by subjecting the early stages to extreme temperatures. The latter has been responsible for the artificial production of some of the extreme forms that are similar in appearance to those caught in the wild. This may give a clue as to the underlying causes for the occurrence of these remarkable insects in the field.

The immense interest in the variation of our British species is best illustrated by the fact that only in this country are there any books devoted almost, if not entirely, to this subject - and these number less than half a dozen.

I felt very pleased and honoured, therefore, when it was suggested that I write this foreword to Alec Harmer's *Variation in British Butterflies*, which has been so beautifully illustrated by our mutual friend Donald Russwurm. I have known Don since the late sixties when he visited me at the Natural History Museum at South Kensington to discuss the choice of specimens for the new 'South' plates that he had been commissioned to paint.

I am of the firm opinion, and many will agree with me, that Don's expertise in the field of illustrating lepidoptera is, without doubt, a perfect example of the watercolourist's art. With his extreme accuracy and delicacy of brushwork he has been able to capture the exact likeness of the living insect. Coupled with this is his speed of execution which over the years has enabled him to paint hundreds - if not thousands - of illustrations for his many friends and, of course, for his own *Aberrations of British Butterflies*. It is in respect of this work that he is perhaps best known.

Don's patience in searching for these varietal forms in the field over many years has been amply rewarded, for one has only to examine the data in the captions to the plates in *South's British Butterflies, Colour Identification Guide to Butterflies of the British Isles* or his own book, to realize the truth of this observation.

I think that *Variation in British Butterflies* together with its delightful and most interesting biography of Don does justice to a very generous friend and lepidopterist.

T. Graham Howarth
T. Graham Howarth
Ferndown, Dorset, *June 1999*

PREFACE

THERE can be few lepidopterists' bookshelves that do not contain a treasured and well-thumbed copy of *The Butterflies of the British Isles* by Richard South. Most likely it was their first serious book on the subject, owned since childhood and a gift, perhaps, from their parents or a favourite uncle or aunt. A measure of its tremendous popularity and influence upon generations of butterfly enthusiasts can be gauged by the fact that it remained in print for nearly seventy years. It is remarkable to think that when it was first published all that time ago, near the turn of the last century, in 1906, Donald Russwurm by then was already two years old. He was sixty-nine when this classic work was eventually revised under the title *South's British Butterflies*, in which he illustrated the adult stages, and he has now celebrated his ninety-fifth birthday! How fitting, then, that the turn of this new century - and indeed millennium - should likewise start with the publication of a book on butterflies, not only illustrated by this well-known artist and collector but also about him - the times he has lived through, his collecting successes, and his achievements during an artistic career that has spanned the past fifty years.

It has been my privilege to know Don Russwurm for some twenty-eight years now. We have spent countless summer days in each other's company in search of elusive aberrations, and many a pleasant evening has been whiled away in deep discussion over captures past and present.

During the early years of our friendship he very kindly accepted a commission from me to complete a number of watercolours of butterfly aberrations and it is these paintings which form the focus of this book. I am pleased that the opportunity has come about whereby this beautiful collection of his work can now be shared with a wider audience to enjoy as much as I have over the past twenty-five years.

Soon after *Aberrations of British Butterflies* by A. D. A. Russwurm was published in 1978, the idea was put forward that a second book should follow. With *Variation in British Butterflies* intended as a companion volume to 'Aberrations', that suggestion has at last been realized.

Readers already familiar with 'South's' or 'Aberrations' will no doubt recognize some of the specimens figured here. Some duplication has been unavoidable owing to the fact that the paintings were carried out about the time 'South's' was published and to some extent were selected from the same source of material. Subsequently, aberrations from the commission were later selected for inclusion in 'Aberrations'. However, with the progress in printing technology in the decades since these two books were published, there is now the opportunity to enjoy these aberrations afresh.

The paintings appear largely in their original format, retaining their original aesthetic appearance. Some minor rationalization and rearrangement have been necessary, but I am pleased to say that the book has benefited as a result. The aberrations originally selected were based largely upon personal choice, with the less variable species and rarer migrants being omitted. In addition, the commission contained four plates of typical specimens and these have been retained, their beauty alone being sufficient justification for inclusion here.

The aberrations featured are among the finest taken over the last century. As habitat loss continues irreversibly, such halcyon days of collecting will not be seen again. Many of the butterflies featured here were taken in the New Forest, once the Mecca for collectors. Sadly, this is no longer the case as commercial exploitation, uncontrolled grazing within the Forest Inclosures and a management policy insensitive and uncaring to the needs of these beautiful insects, have all contributed to their demise.

That this book has been possible is due in no small measure to the efforts of numerous past collectors, amongst them many departed friends, whose time and efforts were devoted to seeking out these rarities. This book, therefore, is in part tribute to them for the legacy they have left for others to enjoy. It is testimony to the dedication of present-day collectors that aberrational treasures still continue to grace the pages of the entomological journals and, just occasionally, new aberrations turn up, confirming the fact that there are still more exciting forms awaiting discovery.

The scientific names used for the British butterflies in this book are from the *Checklist of Lepidoptera recorded from the British Isles*, by J. D. Bradley (1998). Opinions differ as to whether or not English names should begin with a capital letter. My preference has been to use upper case. I have also adopted the practice of using English names throughout the text to assist readers not yet familiar with the scientific names. On the first occasion a species is mentioned in the text, the scientific name and that of the original author or describer are included. With the exception of the use of the letter L as the universally recognized abbreviation for Linnaeus, all other authors' names are given in full.

The nomenclature for the aberrations is from an unpublished synonymic list held at the Natural History Museum, London, entitled *The Aberrational and Subspecific Forms of British Lepidoptera*, by A. L. Goodson and D. K. Read. In compiling this authoritative work they adopted the rules of precedence that govern scientific nomenclature. Although these rules are not strictly applicable below sub-specific status, adherence to the principle of priority provides a constant point of reference from which to work, essential in instances where as many as eight names have been bestowed upon the same aberration! Regrettably though, it has meant that some favourite long-established aberrational names have been displaced. It is a curious fact that whilst some of the most minor forms have been formally described and named, other more outstanding aberrations have not, and so remain as 'ab. nov.' (new aberration).

It should be remembered that gradation exists from the typical insect to the most extreme variety. Some of the aberrations figured here are transitional and perhaps I can do no better than to repeat the words Don used in his Introduction to *Aberrations of British Butterflies* ' ... so that it must sometimes be left to the individual to decide into which category a particular specimen should be placed.'

I hope this compilation of paintings, collections and recollections will find favour not just among aberration devotees and lepidopterists in general, but that it will also appeal to all who share an interest in natural history, the countryside and the skill of the wildlife illustrator.

ACKNOWLEDGEMENTS

I wish to record my thanks and appreciation to everyone who gave assistance, encouragement and support to me during the preparation of this book. If I have inadvertently forgotten to mention anyone, it does not signify that their contribution has been valued any the less. I offer my sincere apologies if any such oversight has occurred.

Karl Bailey has taken the effects of temperature and day length on wing pattern development to a higher plane, achieving the most remarkable results in his experiments. I am grateful to him for the opportunity to borrow from his unpublished notes and material. Over the years, Rupert Barrington has steadily acquired some spectacular aberrations, both in the field and through his breeding achievements; he has been exceptionally fortunate with the Meadow Brown. I have drawn extensively from many of the articles he has generously placed at my disposal.

Don and I are delighted to have included Ian Farwell's photographs, to enrich these pages. They serve as an affectionate reminder of a dear friend and we extend our warmest thanks to Hazel Farwell for their loan. Graham Howarth, in addition to writing the foreword and providing excellent scientific advice, brought several useful references to my attention. Sharon Hutchings kindly came to my assistance whenever my word processing skills ran into difficulties. I am particularly indebted to Michael Majerus, at the Department of Genetics, University of Cambridge. Amidst a busy schedule, he found time to vet the chapters on genetics and his helpful advice and encouragement are very much appreciated.

Throughout our long-standing friendship, Richard Revels has freely shared his exceptional knowledge and experience of butterfly genetics. His reputation as a successful collector, breeder, and wildlife photographer is justly deserved and I am delighted to have been able to incorporate his talents here. I am most grateful to Tom S. Robertson for his published articles on different aspects of butterfly genetics and variation, providing me with a wealth of information to the betterment of the book. Don and I join in thanking Mark Middleton for the constant support he has given throughout this project.

Tony Pickles deserves special mention. We have been close friends and fellow bug-hunters since our schooldays. In addition to his part in arranging the publication of this book and overseeing its financial administration, he volunteered to assist in the laborious task of compiling the bibliography and index, saving me much work and valuable time. He has also contributed towards the book's overall design and content and his extensive library proved to be an indispensable source of innumerable references.

The considerable demands placed upon my time in the preparation of this book over the past year or so has meant neglecting certain family and domestic commitments. Maggie and Arran have shown forbearance, understanding and support at all times; they have my love, respect and gratitude. I should also like to thank my father, Douglas Harmer, for checking the early text drafts and for drawing my attention to some of the finer points of English grammar and punctuation. Carol and John Bartlett are to be congratulated for the fine job they have done in proof reading.

In addition to those persons above who kindly loaned photographs, my appreciation is extended to the following individuals, companies and organizations who generously gave permission for reproduction of material: Bob Gibbons/Natural Image; the Editor, *British Journal of Entomology and Natural History;* the Editor, *The Entomologist's Record and Journal of Variation;* Ian Allan Publishing Ltd.; Natural History Museum, London and David Carter; Royal Society For The Promotion of Nature Reserves; David Wilson.

It is particularly gratifying to have produced this book locally. Don and I are indebted to Printwise of Lymington for the interest and enthusiasm they have shown throughout this project. They have taken the utmost care to ensure that the colour plates are a faithful reproduction of the original paintings. Martin Brewer is to be congratulated for the masterly way in which he has interpreted all ideas and diagrams.

My final acknowledgement must be to Don. Quite simply, without him this book would not have been possible. With his artistic eye for form and detail, he has been closely involved in every stage of production. On the occasions when, for whatever reason, progress has been delayed, he has shown characteristic good humour and understanding.

Although I have gone to considerable lengths to ensure the accuracy of the contents, it is, perhaps, inevitable in a book of this nature that ample opportunity exists for error. I would welcome being advised of any mistakes found, in case a future occasion arises when they may be rectified.

A. S. H.
October 1999

INTRODUCTION

I FIRST met Don Russwurm in May 1971, while I was on a collecting holiday in the New Forest. During earlier trips to the area, I had made the acquaintance of the New Forest natural history photographer, Robin Fletcher, who knew Don. Mentioning to Robin how much I admired the artist's work in *Notes and Views of the Purple Emperor*, he suggested that I wrote to Don. I did so and he replied, kindly inviting me over to Coridon, his Brockenhurst home. That evening, after viewing his impressive collection, he showed me two volumes of butterfly aberrations that he had painted. The extreme nature of the aberrations he had illustrated, together with his wonderful technique and great attention to detail, were an absolute delight. He had recently finished the plates for the new *South's British Butterflies*, and was expecting it to be published that year.

Over a hot night-cap, we arranged to meet again and together over the next few days collected the Marsh Fritillary, *Euphydryas aurinia* (Rottemburg) in Dorset, the Small Pearl-bordered Fritillary, *Boloria selene selene* ([Denis & Schiffermüller]) in Wiltshire, and the Pearl-bordered Fritillary, *Boloria euphrosyne* (L.) in the New Forest. Don's collecting companion, Mark Middleton, joined us on most of these trips. The frontispiece photograph was taken on one of these outings, a hot sunny afternoon in Denny Lodge Inclosure, and Pearl-bordered Fritillaries in good numbers all along the rides, with sometimes two or three competing for the same bugle flower. On those early trips I learnt from Don that to be at all successful in hunting aberrations, a methodical approach to collecting was necessary.

My few days holiday were soon over and as a farewell gift he presented me with four paintings. We discussed the possibility of his accepting a commission from me to which he kindly agreed, suggesting the extremely reasonable fee of £1 per plate. From his volumes we selected the species and aberrations to be figured and the approximate number of plates, the proposal being to complete four a month.

Soon after my return to London, Don wrote telling me he had been very fortunate in obtaining, through his friend Ian Farwell (who worked in the printing department of Kings of Lymington), a stock of the same paper as he had used for the 'South's' plates.

Work on the paintings commenced in September that year and by the end of October the first twenty plates had been completed. These were the Purple Emperor, *Apatura iris* (L.), White Admiral, *Limenitis camilla* (L.), Small Tortoiseshell, *Aglais urticae*, (L.), Painted Lady, *Cynthia cardui* (L.), Peacock, *Inachis io* (L.) and the Large Tortoiseshell, *Nymphalis polychloros* (L.). Don wrote saying that as the quality of the natural lighting had remained particularly good he had taken advantage of it to complete the plates of the Chalk Hill Blue, *Lysandra coridon* (Poda) and Adonis Blue, *Lysandra bellargus* (Rottemburg). It was readily agreed that he could paint them in the order that he considered best. In November, Don wrote suggesting that instead of the number of plates being reduced from seventy-four to sixty to enable them to fit in one volume, as originally proposed, they should now be increased to eighty, and be spread over two volumes.

By early February 1972 the first volume was completed. Work on my paintings was fitted in with other commissions, including one for Major-General C. G. Lipscomb, who required about one hundred of his aberrations to be painted before his collection passed to the Natural History Museum, London.

In April 1973, I visited Don to collect the first eight plates of the second volume, which included the Comma, *Polygonia c-album* (L.), Small Pearl-bordered Fritillary and Pearl-bordered Fritillary. He had received an advance copy of '*South's*' and apart from a few plates, was quite pleased with the publisher's efforts in reproducing his work.

In June 1974, I moved from Kent to live in the New Forest and this coincided with the near completion of the second volume as far as the Grayling, *Hipparchia semele semele* (L.). Finally, in early 1975 the paintings were finished. The additional paintings on Plates: 9, 10, 53 (fig. 3) and 72 were done in 1980, during Don's convalescence at Covertside following a hip replacement operation.

Maggie Fuller, Don Russwurm and Robin Fletcher outside Roe Cottage, New Forest, Autumn 1974.

In addition to his own wonderful collection from which to select specimens for figuring in my commission, Don had been given access to some of the most important private collections of the period, several of these being local to him. What has happened since to these collections? Douglas Bessemer's collection was at Lyndhurst (later sold to the Tring Museum for £6,000); Robert Watson's collection was at Boldre until his death in 1982, when it was bequeathed to the Natural History Museum, London; John Turner's collection (which I was fortunate enough to see shortly before he died in 1975) was sold to the Saruman Museum, eventually to be purchased along with the rest of the Saruman Collection by Worldwide Butterflies. At the sale of this impressive collection in 1991, I was able to purchase three of the specimens that appear in this book: the female Chalk Hill Blue aberration taken by R. L. E. Ford (Plate 24, fig. 8) £100, the melanic Small Pearl-bordered Fritillary captured by V. Penn (Plate 45, figs 5, 6) £260 and the High Brown Fritillary, *Argynnis adippe vulgoadippe* Verity ab. *bronzus* Frohawk (Plate 50, figs 1, 2) for £95. The opportunity was also taken to buy the Black Hairstreak, *Satyrium pruni* (L.) ab. *albofasciata* Tutt, bred by C. N. Hughes in 1907, for £100. This famous insect has been figured in *Varieties of British Butterflies*, by F. W. Frohawk, and *South's British Butterflies*, by T. G. Howarth.

I ORIGINALLY considered having these paintings properly bound soon after their completion in 1975, but delayed doing so for several reasons. To accompany each plate Don had typed a separate page of data including the names of those aberrations he was familiar with. However, many of the specimens had still to be named and the difficulties in being able to accomplish this task soon became evident during a visit to the Natural History Museum with Don in 1976. Between assisting him in the selection of specimens from the National Collection for figuring in *Aberrations of British Butterflies*, I made a tentative start at identifying the aberrations in my paintings, using the Collection for reference. It soon became obvious that completing the job was going to be a slow and expensive business, entailing repeated trips to the Museum. With so many additional names and other information to be included, it was not going to be a practical proposition to amend Don's original type work. I decided to shelve the project until such times as these problems could be resolved. The acquisition of a computer in 1997 provided the answer.

I was now in a position to fulfil not only all my initial objectives, but also to consider including a short explanation as to how the paintings came to be commissioned and the part they had played in the publication of *Aberrations of British Butterflies*. Other ideas followed. Don's long and successful career both as a collector and as one of the country's foremost butterfly artists had never been documented. Recalling his amusing collecting anecdotes, I decided that they should not go unrecorded. I wanted to recall the times when some of his wonderful aberrations were taken, evoking memories of seasons and places long ago; to recapture those heady moments of joyous disbelief when finally a prize is captured.

The opportunity to produce this short biography was pursued and in the Spring of 1997, Don and I sat down together and began getting it all down on paper.

While arranging to have the finished manuscript and data professionally printed, it was suggested by Tony Pickles that I should take the opportunity to have the paintings electronically copied, in the event that someday they might be published. Although I followed his advice, the prospect of this happening seemed remote due to the enormous costs of publishing, and possible limited demand for a book covering such a specialized subject. Copies of the manuscript were circulated by Don amongst his friends; the favourable comments that came back were encouraging and requests for further copies followed.

Then around Christmas 1998, quite unexpectedly, Don informed me that he wanted to see the short biography and paintings published as a companion volume to *Aberrations of British Butterflies* and was prepared to finance the project. His only proviso was that the original artistic layout of the paintings should be preserved.

Although suddenly being presented with a host of daunting new challenges and responsibilities, I realized this unexpected turn of events opened up new, exciting possibilities. In particular, publication meant that the biography could now be illustrated, adding enormously to its interest. Furthermore, I saw an opportunity to include a brief explanation of the underlying genetic principles that determine many of the wonderful aberrations Don had figured, providing the reader with a greater understanding into their origins, and an enhanced appreciation. Besides complementing the paintings in this way, my intention was that any information and advice would be kept very much at a level where they would be of practical benefit to those interested in the breeding of butterflies to obtain aberrations.

In the half century or more that has passed since E. B. Ford's brilliant book *Butterflies* was published, there have been further discoveries in butterfly genetics and numerous contributions on the subject published in the entomological journals. It seemed logical to consolidate at least some of this knowledge here.

Don Russwurm, Coridon, Brockenhurst, June 1971.

PART ONE:

A Biography

Chapter One

An Englishman Abroad

ALEXANDER DONALD ABBOT RUSSWURM was born on June 11th 1904 in Guildford, Surrey, to Ethel and Alexander Russwurm, and was the eldest of three children. He was still young when the family moved to Leighton Buzzard, Bedfordshire, where his father had been appointed as manager to the local branch of the Westminster Bank.

Don's interest in butterflies started at about the age of twelve when his father captured a couple of butterflies in the garden one day. Although not an active collector himself, he seemed to have some knowledge on almost every subject, and he showed his son how to set them using an improvised setting-board constructed from two matchboxes. Don was captivated and took up collecting, thus beginning a love of these beautiful insects that has lasted throughout his life.

His schooldays at Bletchley and Dunstable were on the whole uneventful, and finishing school at sixteen he joined the Eastern Telegraph Company where, after two years of intensive training, he qualified as a submarine cable telegraphist. At this point I shall let Don describe the wonderful experiences he had as a young man travelling abroad on foreign service during the early part of his career.

'I WAS appointed to the cable station at Carcavellos, in Portugal, situated seventeen miles north of Lisbon on the Atlantic coast. I had by now acquired sufficient knowledge of Lepidoptera to become very excited at seeing many British rarities flying here in abundance. To name a few: the Continental Swallowtail, *Papilio machaon gorganus* Fruhstorfer was common; the southern European Brimstone, Cleopatra, *Gonepteryx cleopatra* (L.), similar to our native species except for a bright orange area which spreads across the forewings and only occurs in the male; the magnificent Cardinal, *Argynnis pandora* (Denis & Schiffermüller) found clustering in numbers on the thistles near the sea-shore; many species of Lycaenidae, including the Long-tailed Blue, *Lampides boeticus* (L.); various Satyrids, relatives of our Marbled White, *Melanargia galathea serena* Verity. The Bath White, *Pontia daplidice* (L.) was also abundant with its fairly close relative, the Green-striped White, *Euchloe belemia* (Esper). Some moths were also conspicuous: the Spurge Hawk-moth, *Hyles euphorbiae* (L.) was bred from a number of larvae found feeding, and the Striped Hawk-moth, *Hyles livornica* (Esper), captured at dusk when flying around some flowering bushes.

The staff at the cable station numbered about eighty and so with six tennis courts and a nine hole golf course, life was very enjoyable. Some time had to be passed in the cable office but this was rarely allowed to interfere with these delectable pastimes.

After fourteen months I was transferred to Marseille. Travelling north from Lisbon on the Sud Express, we changed trains at the frontier (where the track gauge changed from the extra width of Spain and Portugal). At Bordeaux we left the luxurious express and travelled across France on a cold night, arriving at Marseille in a snow-storm. At the first sign of Spring the Camberwell Beauty, *Nymphalis antiopa* (L.) appeared from hibernation but most were faded and worn, so no examples were kept.

Although my stay in Marseille was fairly brief, as I left for Egypt after only eight months, a number of interesting butterflies were seen nonetheless. The Scarce Swallowtail, *Iphiclides podalirius* (L.) was encountered, a very rare visitor to Britain but common enough in the South of France; the Southern Comma, *Polygonia egea* (Cramer), of which only one specimen was seen and taken, and a very large Satyrid, the Great Banded Grayling, *Kanetisa circe* (Fabricius), looking more like an outsize White Admiral, with its black wings crossed by a single white band. This was quite common but had an unfortunate habit of settling on tree trunks, making capture difficult. The Camberwell Beauties began to appear two days before my departure for Egypt but were so fresh and lively that they could not be caught. Finally, one other species deserves mention, the Mazarine Blue, *Cyaniris semiargus* (Rottemburg), which flew in numbers over the lawns surrounding our quarters.

I sailed from Marseille in June 1924 on the P&O liner *Kaiser-i-hind*. At that time reputed to be the oldest ship in the Line and also the fastest, she had been known to arrive in port as much as twenty-four hours ahead of schedule. There were rumours that this was to be her last voyage before being broken up. Our cabin situated somewhere between the boiler room and the propellers, gave every indication that the ship had already shaken herself to pieces! However, we reached Port Said safely and boarded a train of the very efficient Egyptian State Railways bound for Alexandria. The railway was originally built by engineers from our own Great Western Railway, of which there were many indications, for example, the design of the stations and the deep-green livery of the engines with their brass-rimmed chimneys. Very little entomology was possible in Egypt, particularly in Alexandria, the town being surrounded on three sides by desert and on the fourth by sea. Whilst playing golf one day I did see a specimen of the Plain Tiger, *Danaus chrysippus* (L.) fly across the course. A native of south-west Asia and east Africa, it is also sometimes known as the African Monarch.

After twelve months I was transferred to Suez where I remained for another eight months; a very different life from the town just left and much more enjoyable, and as before, a very large staff and our own tennis courts and golf course. Golf here was a different story, the fairway being composed of hard-baked mud laced with salt, so a 'topped' drive would run for miles jumping and bouncing off various obstacles. The tennis courts were good and I reached the final of the open singles only to lose the match after holding a number of match points; an unfortunate habit this, as history repeated itself some years later in the final at Zanzibar. All I found here was a small species of Skipper on the banks of the Sweet Water Canal.

This completes my experience of the natural history of Egypt, but before leaving Suez mention should be made of the colours when the sun set behind the mountains and shafts of light in green and orange spread over the sky. Anyone who has not actually seen it would find it difficult to believe. I painted this scene many times.

With the final two years spent in Aden, my term of five years foreign service was completed. At Aden, where the earth's crust is thinner than anywhere else in the world, there is a rift in it which runs from the British coaling station of Perim, at the southern end of the Red Sea, through Aden and on into the Indian Ocean. The oppressive heat and humidity of the region are such that one appears to be living in a steaming kettle. From the sea Aden looks like a dead world with not a trace of foliage or any other form of life. Strangely enough, there are butterflies in Aden, as a number of shrubs and other low growing plants are to be found in the valleys leading down to the sea. A notably abundant species was a Nymphalid, the False Plain Tiger, *Hypolimnas misippus* (L.). The male is black with a large white spot on each wing, which is shot with purple; the female brown, somewhat resembling a Danaid. Another genus which was well represented was *Colotis*, many of the species resembling small Clouded Yellows.

This was a difficult two years in a very unhealthy and uncomfortable climate so that I was more than ready for a well-earned six month's leave. I sailed for home aboard the P&O liner *Ranpura*, a fine ship. Two of her sister ships, the *Rajputana* and *Rawalpindi* were, I believe, lost during the war.

My second term abroad began with a brief but very pleasant return to Suez. I sailed from the King George V dock at Tilbury on the very old P&O liner *Kashgar*, although the voyage out to Port Said was comfortable enough. From there by train down to Suez where, after only four months, I embarked again, this time on the French liner *Explorateur Grandidier*, travelling through the Red Sea and down the east coast of Africa to the cable station at Zanzibar, for what was to be one of the longest and most enjoyable appointments of my career. A much smaller station, the staff numbered no more than thirty-five, this was a pleasant change after the high-speed working on main line cables previously experienced. The mess and office were housed in the same building and situated on the sea-shore. The brightly-lit office with its twenty-four hour service acted as an excellent moth-trap. Many times I was called up during the night by one of the staff to come down and box some magnificent Hawk-moth or Emperor.

The island of Zanzibar is sixty miles long and twenty wide, the main industry being the plantations of cloves, the spice used not only for flavouring apple tarts but also widely in the chemical industry. The strong scent would permeate the whole island at times and for years afterwards, when stationed in the London office, I thought I could detect the scent of cloves every time I walked past the Zanzibar wireless circuit! It would be almost impossible to describe all the butterflies found on this tropical island just below the Equator. The majority of the African families were represented, including five species of the Swallowtail. My favourite of these was the beautiful *Papilio nireus* (L.), with jet-black wings crossed with a band of iridescent blue-green; a very strong flyer, it rarely seemed to settle, so a capture eluded me for some time. It seems ironic to have to relate that on setting out with my net on the morning after my arrival, the first butterfly I netted was a Painted Lady. However, I was soon kept busy collecting my short series of more than one hundred species.

Some of the magnificent moths deserve a chapter to themselves. The first to be described is the magnificent day-flying moth *Chrysiridia croesus* Gerstaecker, very abundant in some years whereas at other times it is absent for long periods. During my first year I saw one specimen only, which I failed to capture. But the second year they came in thousands. Arriving early in the afternoon, they were to be seen either hanging from the trees or else flying about, their brilliant wings with all the colours of the rainbow set against a jet-black ground colour glittering in the sunshine. My office looked out on to a square, where the trees in it were filled with this magnificent spectacle. "I expect you'll be wanting some of those," said my supervisor very understandingly, excusing me from duty for the rest of the afternoon so that I could catch my series. I only came across one specimen of the closely related *Chrysiridia riphearia* Drury. It had flown into the captain's cabin on one of the cable ships coming up from Durban. Finding the moth on his pillow, he summoned the ship's doctor who promptly dispatched it with chloroform. I was duly presented with the specimen when the ship docked in Zanzibar. Two very large Emperor moths should be mentioned: *Nudaurelia zambezina* Walker, coloured in shades of grey and olive-green, with the four 'eye' spots that are characteristic of this family, and *Nudaurelia said* Oberthür, with similar markings, but coloured in reddish-brown. Both moths were quite common and often flew into the brightly-lit cable office at night. My first experience of the Oleander Hawk-moth, *Daphnis nerii* (L.) was served up with my breakfast one morning when one of the mess boys brought the specimen to me in a champagne tumbler! Another beautiful Sphingid, the Verdant Hawk-moth, *Euchloron megaera* (L.), had been captured before my arrival and kept in cold storage, my reputation having preceded me. A fine insect with bright emerald-green forewings and yellow hindwings banded with black, I only took one other specimen during my stay. Shortly before sailing for home, I visited the Isle of Pemba some miles north of Zanzibar where I took further species of the Acraeidae, an East African family of smallish brown butterflies. After more than two years I left on the British India liner SS *Matiana*. She had the same khaki upper works and black funnels as the P&O, which was an associate line.

My foreign service had now come to an end and on my return home in 1932 I was appointed to Electra House, the Company's office in Moorgate, London.'

O N RETURNING to England, Don lived with his mother and sisters in Bushey, Hertfordshire. Family commitments, combined with a demanding job involving a weekly rota of day and night shifts, meant his spare time was severely restricted and his collecting had to be put aside, so instead he concentrated on his landscape oil-painting and his interest in railways.

As a small boy living in Leighton Buzzard he had been fascinated by the trains on the London & North Western line, with their black engines lined with silver and white and the 'spilt milk' and purple brown livery of the coaches. Later, during his two years of training in London he would spend hours visiting the various stations and termini. Paddington for the Great Western, Euston for the London & North Western, King's Cross for the Great Northern, and Waterloo for the London & South Western. Many years later, when Don was working at Electra House, the company received a visit from a 'big noise' in the London Midland Scottish Railway. In return for being shown round the Company's operations, the gentleman invited the traffic superintendent and Don to spend a morning in the railway sheds at Camden Town. The foreman cleaner apologised to them for the dirty condition of a 'Princess Royal' class which had recently emerged from the sheds. He was unable to clean her as she was due to go out again in half an hour and that was the trouble he explained - they were never in for long enough. Don vividly remembers that while standing on the track busily absorbed in taking photographs, a 'Patriot' class engine behind him waiting to get back into the shed, emitted a piercing whistle. He nearly leapt out of his skin!

He became a keen railway model enthusiast developing and modifying his own 'OO' gauge layout. A regular visitor to the model railway exhibitions held at Westminster Hall, he also contributed articles and photographs to several of the railway magazines. One of the articles that featured some of his oil paintings of trains is included here. In all, he completed about twenty pictures of engines in their pre-Grouping colours prior to 1923, when the big four companies were formed.

Don's prize-winning photograph in a competition run by the magazine *Railways*. Claud Hamilton locomotive ex Great Eastern Railway, rebuilt with enlarged boiler for the L.N.E.R. From *Railways*, May 1940.
(By kind permission of Ian Allan Publishing Ltd)

The *Princess Royal* passing over the water troughs at Bushey during her first week of service. She was the first Pacific class to be placed into service on the L.M.S. Published in *Railway Magazine* circa 1935.
Photo: A. D. A. Russwurm and reproduced by kind permission.

Modelling Items.

★

A brief description by A. D. A. Russwurm of his "OO" gauge layout.

THE PHOTOGRAPHS reproduced in this short article show a series of locomotives forming the stud of a free lance system which has running powers over my L.M.S. layout; I have called this line the Colne Valley Railway, although it has no connection with the old line of that name (now part of the L.N.E.R.), in fact locomotives and passenger stock are painted in Caledonian blue.

All these models were constructed from the original Hornby "Dublo." tank loco, only one of which is running in its original form, this can be seen with a rebuild which was fitted with a Belpaire fire-box and boiler of smaller dimensions; the resultant taller chimney and steam dome gives the model an entirely new appearance.

With regard to the eight coupled goods only the main frame remains, tank sides and boiler having been entirely sawn away and the new body built on to the frame which still fits on to the mechanism in the way originally intended.

The Beyer-Garratt belongs to the L.M.S. section and was a bigger proposition, two 0—6—2T after further and still more drastic treatment with the hacksaw are used; only one unit is alive, the other had not given very satisfactory performance during its period of active service, so the worm was removed to give free running; the boiler section is built on to a brass plate which rests over the two chassis and swivels from the screws holding the bodies to the mechanisms, the engine thus being flexible to negotiate any curve down to a 2 foot radius. The model follows the L.M.S. 2—6—0 + 0—6—2 type in general proportions, but naturally does not claim to be a scale model of the prototype, the cylinders are soldered to a brass plate which fits over the chassis. I have had little success in soldering the alloy used by "Hornby" although others claim to have overcome this difficulty; the addition of a revolving coal bunker is under consideration.

An 0—6—4T with Belpaire fire-box rebuilt cabin and extended coal bunker is not shown here, the fixing of a four-wheeled bogey in place of the pony truck presented no difficulty.

The extremely smooth and quiet running of these mechanisms encourages one to exploit them to the fullest extent and I have found that double-heading can be operated with great success—without any jerking through lack of synchronisation.

To the skilled craftsman this method of building locomotives must seem a rather unorthodox practice but lack of workshop facilities has necessitated making the best use of all available material.

A comprehensive view of the locomotive yard is shown in the top photograph, where a Baltic 4—6—4T, 0—6—0T, and a repainted Southern Lord Nelson can be seen, but these are not under review in this article, which is intended primarily to show the exploitation of the Hornby "OO" tank. A plan of the railway will be given next month, together with further pictures of the locomotives.

Don was a regular contributor to the magazine *Railways*. From *Railways*, January 1942. (By kind permission of Ian Allan Publishing Ltd.)

The above four pictures are miniature reproductions of some excellent oil paintings by A. D. A. Russwurm. The artist has done considerable work in general landscapes in both water and oil colours, and he decided some months ago to experiment with railway scenes following upon remarks in 'RAILWAYS,' and our esteemed contemporary the "Model Railway News," concerning railways as a subject for the painter. The half-tone reproductions do not convey adequately the beauty of the colouring or the general effect when the pictures are viewed from a little distance. It should be noted that these paintings are direct on to the canvas and are in this sense genuine oil paintings. It is to be hoped that the artist will develop this medium as conditions allow. The trains depicted are the S.R. Waterloo—Bournemouth express; the "Irish Mail" of the L.M.S.R. passing along the North Wales Coast; a G.W.R. express arriving at Paddington; a passenger train on the L.N.E.R. hauled by an ex-G.N.R. "Atlantic" locomotive.

From *Railways*, May 1940. (By kind permission of Ian Allan Publishing Ltd.)

The Depression of the early thirties was a difficult time, the industrial slump having brought nearly all foreign trade to a standstill and the possibility of redundancy was ever present. The introduction of new technology by the company meant Don had to master new skills if he was to keep his job.

The threat of war in 1938 heralded a change in fortunes for his employers. Security became a vital concern and messages sent via submarine cables could not be intercepted. Consequently telegraphists were once more in demand and placed on the reserved occupation list. Soon after the war started Don began working permanent night duty to avoid travelling during the air-raids. Working alternate nights, commencing at five in the afternoon and finishing at eight the following morning, he often had to pick his way between burning buildings and clamber over the firemens' leaking hoses when there had been an air-raid during the night. Additionally, once a week an extra eight hour shift starting at ten in the evening had to be worked for which overtime was paid. With the restrictions imposed by the war and only one week's annual leave throughout this period, there was very little time left for leisure. This pattern of working lasted throughout the war, but afterwards, finding that it was compatible with collecting, Don continued with the arrangement until his retirement in 1959.

Electra House survived many air–raids until finally an incendiary bomb fell on the roof of the adjoining Tower Chambers, the resulting fire quickly spreading to Electra House. By this time operations had already been transferred to another building of the same name on the Thames Embankment, near the Temple Underground Station. A bomb-proof room known as the 'Fortress' was constructed inside the building, and a red light would come on in the room whenever there was an air-raid overhead. Don was off duty at the time when the Chairman's office suffered a direct hit from the only flying bomb to come over that night. Four people sheltering in the basement area were killed by falling masonry. Don recalls seeing the very first flying bomb to come over in June 1944 as he was going off duty at six in the morning. People were standing in the street cheering, thinking it was an enemy fighter plane being brought down. Several more arrived by eight o'clock and by the evening warnings were being given out over the wireless.

Photos of Don in his younger days are rare. Taken circa 1950. Photo: I. G. Farwell. (By kind permission of Hazel Farwell.)

Don had several narrow escapes during these years. He was at work when the family home at Bushey was bombed out - the target being the railway that ran alongside the house. His family decided to move to Kimbolton in Huntingdonshire, and Don moved to Notting Hill Gate, where he stayed for the next ten years. On one occasion, having just spread some of his landscape paintings around his room, he heard the scream of bombs followed by a big explosion. He quickly packed his suitcase thinking he would be evacuated, but the air-raid warden informed him that the bombs had fallen in the next street and demolished four houses. Another time, while he was at St. Pancras Station, a flying bomb cut out overhead. Everyone else threw themselves down, but Don, experiencing total paralysis, remained standing, unable to move a muscle. Fortunately, the bomb landed about a mile away.

Although it was not possible to do much collecting during these difficult times, his entomological memories of the period include each day on his way to work passing by the colour plates for E. B. Ford's *Butterflies* which because of wartime delays had been on display in the publisher's window in Arundel Street during the period of the War.

For the last fifteen years of his career his time was spent in a clerical capacity checking overseas cablegrams for accuracy. After leaving Notting Hill Gate he then moved to Streatham, where he stayed a further four years before moving to Sanderstead in Surrey. During these years he was a regular visitor to the orchestral concerts at the Festival Hall and the operas at Covent Garden, the latter included some complete performances of Wagner's *Der Ring des Nibelungen,* which he particularly enjoyed. In those post war years he had the distinction of being Watkins & Doncaster's final customer at their premises in the Strand. Richard Ford sold him a packet of black pins before the shop closed in 1956 to make way for redevelopment.

In 1959, the day he retired, he moved down to Coridon, in Brockenhurst, which he had had built. He was then able to devote his time fully to collecting and painting butterflies.

Now, forty years later, Don is still happily retired there, dividing his time between the occasional painting, watching his favourite sports, cricket and tennis, on television and listening to his large collection of classical music. After a lifetime of listening Don considers his favourite composer to be Brahms because, in his opinion, he has the 'greatest resources of entertainment'. Beethoven, Mozart, Haydn, Elgar, Schubert and Dvorak are also among his favourites.

Over the years Don's enthusiasm and interest in butterflies, together with his helpful and generous nature and gracious and unassuming manner, have resulted in the making of many long-lasting friendships. Like many others, I shall always be grateful to him for his encouragement and guidance, and for the generous hospitality he has always shown me. At Christmas the strings of cards hung across his living room reflect the affection and esteem in which he is held.

Coridon is never short of visitors. Don and Mark are kept busy entertaining their many entomological friends, and in recent years Don has been able to renew his long-standing friendship with Graham Howarth, who is now a regular visitor. Although Don is no longer able to attend the British Entomological and Natural History Society's Annual Exhibition in London, after the post-exhibition meal back at Coridon - something of a tradition now - he is still as keen as ever to hear how the season has gone and to see and learn about the latest captures.

Chapter Two

'We Go Whatever the Weather'

A s might be expected, collecting became something of an anticlimax for Don after the excitement of the tropics, until he developed an interest in varieties and aberrations. Thus, for a time, little collecting was done. The general economic crisis, followed by the war itself, were further contributing factors. During the latter period of the war, however, he often visited his mother at Kimbolton and came to discover nearby Tilbrook Wood for himself. His sister Anne had found the White-letter Hairstreak, *Satyrium w-album* (Knoch) swarming there and had managed to catch two, which she sent to him. It was a species he had not taken and eventually he was able to go there himself and take his series. The wood proved to be a real gold-mine, supporting thirty-five species of butterflies including the Silver-washed Fritillary, *Argynnis paphia* (L.), Dark Green Fritillary, *Argynnis aglaja* (L.) and White Admiral. On one particular occasion, he recalled finding a male Meadow Brown, *Maniola jurtina insularis* Thomson, paired with a female Dark Green Fritillary.

During the war, and afterwards, he was a frequent house-guest of a colleague, a keen astronomer who lived in Plaistow, Sussex, and owned a twenty-acre wood. One visit in particular was at the invitation of this friend to watch a solar eclipse through his telescope. Wandering around the wood afterwards in the semi-gloom, Don saw what he took to be a geometer moth flying across the ride. It turned out to be his first encounter with the Wood White, *Leptidea sinapis sinapis* (L.). His first Brown Hairstreak, *Thecla betulae* (L.), a fresh female, was also captured there while he was taking tea with his friends on the lawn. He later bred his series from larvae beaten from the blackthorn bushes behind Balmer Lawn in the New Forest.

His friend had a young nephew of about eight years old who had asked Don what he would give him if he found a butterfly that he did not have. Don's offer was a year's pocket money. Soon afterwards the lad sent Don a male Large Tortoiseshell he had found hibernating in the garden shed. Don got away with paying out ten shillings!

During these years, Don's interest in variation gradually developed and when the war finally ended he was then able to spend more time collecting and, in particular, searching for aberrations. By swapping his shifts around he was often able to get away for up to three days at a time.

I n the late 1940s, whilst travelling by train during a visit to Box Hill, Surrey, Don passed by a large wood which, on further investigation a few days later, proved to be Ashstead Wood. There he found the Small Pearl-bordered Fritillary in great abundance in the damp areas near the railway track and, on the ground higher up, the Pearl-bordered Fritillary was in such swarms that they were having to fight for ground over the bugle flowers. Also present were the High Brown Fritillary and the

White Admiral, and Don remembers, with a degree of embarrassment, catching and releasing some Purple Hairstreaks, *Neozephyrus quercus* (L.), only to discover later that they had been the subtle aberration ab. *flavimaculatus* Lienard. Being so close to London it soon became one of his favourite collecting haunts. Unfortunately, the proximity of Ashstead Wood to the capital had a down side, being regularly ravaged by fires, often started by the Easter picnickers who invaded this beauty spot every year.

Don is well known for the generosity he extends to other collectors, whether it be information or hospitality, and he recollects that Ashstead was once the cause of his being rebuked for this commendable trait. It was in 1947 at Riddlesdown in Surrey, and he had struck up a conversation with a young man, still in Royal Air Force uniform, and employed as a greenkeeper on the local golf course. Noticing Don's net he explained that they shared a mutual interest in butterflies. When Don told him of his recent capture of a white Pearl-bordered Fritillary (ab. *pallida* Spuler, *South's British Butterflies*: Plate 25, fig. 12) at Ashstead Wood, the young man replied that he thought such things only existed on coloured plates in books. Meeting up again a few days later, upon being told that he, too, had now taken the same aberration, Don congratulated him. Later, when recounting the story to another collector with less sporting instincts, Don was soundly told off for giving away the information. Typically, Don's reply was 'Good luck to him - that's why I told him.'

That same summer was to be an incredible time for migrant butterflies and helped to rekindle Don's interest in collecting. While on a week's holiday with his mother at Seaford, Sussex, he discovered a piece of rough ground next to a roadside cutting upon which a clump of lucerne was growing. Glancing over the area he spotted a male Pale Clouded Yellow, *Colias hyale* (L.) which had flown up and swiftly netted it. Thereafter, he patrolled the spot every day, eventually capturing nine males in total. Several female Pale Clouded Yellows were also later taken amongst the swarms of the Clouded Yellow, *Colias croceus* (Geoffroy) that arrived shortly afterwards. Returning from Seaford Head one morning he saw a lovely fresh female Pale Clouded Yellow feeding on some flowers in a front garden - an absolute sitter. Just at that moment a door opened and the owner emerged. Don's nerve failed and he crept away, his net still underneath his coat.

Fifty years on Don can still vividly remember those wonderful captures on the setting boards, drying in the airing cupboard, and looking at them every day, wondering if it had all really happened.

M ANY of Don's early collecting trips involved another great passion in his life, travel by steam train. Not having a car, a great number of his expeditions had to be planned around train time-tables. Contributing to the magazine *Nature Lover* in 1948 (the motto Don quotes in that article has been used as the title for this chapter), he wrote: '…in the hope of adding the Chequered Skipper, *Carterocephalus palaemon* (Pallas) to my cabinet, I left the Flying Scotsman at Peterborough and changed on to a local train. After a further journey of half an hour I was set down at the small wayside station of Wakerley and Barrowden (three trains a day, I believe). Following the directions given to me, I quickly located the wood. The sun had just appeared after an overcast morning and the attractive little butterflies were soon in flight in all directions; they were very agile, being almost as rapid in their movements as the Silver-spotted Skipper, *Hesperia comma* (L.). During periods when the sun was obscured a few specimens were taken at rest on the flowers of bugle, but this proved slow and back-breaking work.' He quickly managed to take his series and be on time for the return train home. Another Skipper - this time the Lulworth Skipper, *Thymelicus acteon* (Rottemburg) - involved catching the 5.20a.m. train from Waterloo to Wareham, Dorset, and thence travelling by taxi to Lulworth Cove, where Don took his series well before mid-morning.

In pursuit of the Heath Fritillary, *Melitaea athalia* (Rottemburg) at Blean, Kent, he had booked a room for three nights in Canterbury, but quickly cancelled the accommodation after the first day, such was the extraordinary abundance of the butterfly. On the station platform afterwards, he met another collector, and they journeyed back to London together. Don noticed that his travelling companion was in very high spirits throughout the journey, only to discover later that the reason for his good mood was an ab. *cymothoë* Bertolini he had in a pill box in his pocket. A few years later, having arranged to meet Ewart Bolton at Blean, Don got the dates confused and consequently failed to turn up. Whilst waiting at the bus stop by the side of the road, fuming over the delay and Don's non-appearance, Bolton picked up a most extreme example of this same aberration.

'I'VE GOT THEM!', read the telegram Don received in late May of 1949 from his friend Major Noel Thomas, who was staying at Great Yarmouth. As pre-arranged, Don duly reported sick, travelled up to Norfolk and the following day they set out in search of the Swallowtail, *Papilio machaon britannicus* Seitz, near Potter Heigham.

'In the most appalling weather, with deluges of rain between fitful gleams of watery sunshine, we trudged a mile and a half through the mud on the Norfolk Broads along Candlewick Dyke hoping to add a few specimens of this magnificent butterfly to our collections. Mention might be made of a ferocious looking bull which pawed the ground and snorted furiously each time we passed. Fortunately he seemed to regard the two-foot wide dyke which separated us as an insuperable barrier.

Standing on a flowery bank, with a very cool wind blowing across the flat country, we surveyed the rain-soaked landscape and agreed that it seemed far removed from butterfly life. However, before long, a break in the clouds produced a gleam of sunshine and within a few minutes I counted eleven of these beautiful insects within a radius of a few yards. Further specimens were seen during a brief sunny spell in the afternoon, but the next day a steady down pour put an end to the expedition.' Don ended up catching the cold that he had used as an excuse for reporting sick.

Returning the following year, he captured a male Swallowtail, with the yellow markings on the forewings greatly reduced (Plate 3).

It was generally believed that the very strong colony of the Chalk Hill Blue at Royston Heath, Hertfordshire, had not survived the ploughing up of the slope during the war. However, in the early 1950s, Don found there was still enough undisturbed habitat and Chalk Hill Blues, especially ab. *semisyngrapha* Tutt, to excite the collector. Once, after a hot day collecting at Royston, he fell asleep on the platform while waiting for the train home. This caused a certain amount of concern amongst the station staff as only the day before they had discovered a dead passenger on the train and thought that they had another one on their hands.

Porthcurno, Cornwall, was a regular holiday haunt of Don's and shortly after the war he caught his first Clouded Yellow form *helice* Hübner at nearby Nanchisal Bay.

Don was not to be so lucky, though, with Cornwall's most famous butterfly. In the early 1950s, Ted Ratcliff, a fellow collector whom Don had first met on holiday at Sandown, Isle of Wight, in 1949, informed him that he had found the Large Blue, *Maculinea arion eutyphron* (Fruhstorfer) in hundreds, in the combes between Bude and Hartland Quay. Unfortunately, Don was unable to get down there that year, and subsequent trips to the West Country to obtain a short series for himself were not successful, each time the weather defeating him. Instead, he had to be content with the specimens that he had purchased near the end of the war from The Butterfly Farm, in Bexley, Kent. The old gentleman, L. W. Newman, had shown him a whole store-box of Large Blues, saying that he had taken them all because the field they had been in was about to be ploughed up. Don remembers at the time Hugh Newman coming over and mentioning that his father was not very conversant with prices and that they would be about 2/6d each.

Don's search for the Black Hairstreak took him to Monks Wood in Huntingdonshire where, despite poor weather conditions, he took two fresh specimens. Later, in 1952, staying at Oriel College at Oxford with Hamish Cole, a medical student he had met at Royston, they found it in Hell Coppice. Whilst at Oxford, they visited St. John's College to look at the series in the Hope Collection. A visit to the same locality the following year found the wood razed to the ground and the colony exterminated.

THE NEW FOREST has always figured prominently in Don's collecting and several summer holidays were spent there after the war, staying at the Crown Hotel in Lyndhurst. Modern collectors cannot begin to visualize the sheer abundance of butterflies that used to be in the New Forest; many entomological journals contain articles that bear testimony to a paradise long since lost. Don remembers a time when the forest rides were filled with flowers and bushes of bramble blossom in abundance. At that time the Parkhill area was a gold mine for the Silver-washed Fritillary; his female somatic mosaic with areas of form *valesina* Esper and white markings on the forewings (Plate 59, fig. 3) was taken there as she was basking on a thistle. Earlier in the season the Small Pearl-bordered Fritillary would be swarming over the grassy rides feeding at the flowers, to be followed soon after by the High Brown Fritillary nectaring on the brambles. In 1959, when Don retired to Brockenhurst, he found all the large fritillaries in swarms, but the following year he remembers their numbers fell drastically and never recovered. By the late 1970s, the High Brown Fritillary was to disappear altogether.

This serious and rapid decline of all woodland butterflies in the New Forest was the result of a number of factors and the subject has been well-documented in entomological literature.

In addition to Parkhill, other favourite New Forest haunts of Don's included: Roe Inclosure, where, in 1964, he captured the melanic Small Pearl-bordered Fritillary figured on Plate 46, figs 1, 2; Rhinefield, which was only a short cycle ride from his home and a good spot for the Silver-studded Blue, *Plebejus argus argus* (L.) in early July; Fritham, and Pignal Inclosure. The magnificent examples of ab. *lanceolata* Shipp in the Ringlet, *Aphantopus hyperantus* (L.) on Plate 83, figs 3, 4 (Plate 35, figs 7, 8 in *Aberrations of British Butterflies*) were both captured in July 1958 at Fritham by Don and his friend Cecil Haxby. Don recalls the two of them walking down the slope at Fritham and something flying up behind Cecil. It was quickly netted by Don and turned out to be one of the finest wild males of *lanceolata* ever taken.

The melanic female Pearl-bordered Fritillary on Plate 47, figs 5, 6 (*South's British Butterflies*: Plate 25, fig. 14) was taken in Pignal Inclosure in 1964 as she was resting on the ground in full sun with her wings expanded like a set specimen. Douglas Bessemer, who lived a few miles away in Lyndhurst, came over to see it on the setting board that same afternoon. He often came over to pick Don up in order to go collecting in the Forest together. According to Don, Bessemer would either be waving his net wildly about in the air in the middle of the ride or else telling stories that were years out of date. Not surprisingly perhaps, very few aberrations bear his labels. One of the few specimens to do so was a Silver-studded Blue. Collecting with his wife one day and both happening to spot the same insect - each from a different direction - a mild argument ensued as to the actual sex of the insect. The matter was finally settled when the butterfly was eventually netted and found to be a gynandromorph!

The male Pearl-bordered Fritillary ab. *tatrica* Aigner shown on Plate 47, fig. 8 (*Aberrations of British Butterflies*: Plate 23, fig. 1) was also taken in Pignal in 1971. Don first spotted it sitting on a dandelion on the other side of a gate, but by the time he had opened and closed it the insect had flown on; however, it was quickly captured a few yards away.

A trip to Pignal Inclosure with his friend Les Young in July 1965 secured the lovely Small Tortoiseshell ab. *semiichnusoides* Pronin figured on Plate 39, figs 3, 4 (*Aberrations of British Butterflies*: Plate 18, fig. 1). Don was stalking it when it flew towards Les who made a wild swipe with his net and missed, whereupon the insect flew back to Don and settled on the ground in front of him. Very sportingly, Les insisted that they should return home straightaway as he did not want Don to carry such a marvellous aberration around all day in the heat. In that same week Don also took the two ab. *obliterae* Robson & Gardner of the White Admiral figured on Plate 31 (*South's British Butterflies*: Plate 19, fig. 2). A further three specimens of this aberration were subsequently taken by him at Ashurst. He had already dismantled his net when he spotted the last one basking near a gate; it patiently waited while he hurriedly reassembled his net.

His own garden in Brockenhurst has also proved to be a gold-mine over the years. Unfortunately, a bilateral gynandromorph Comma eluded capture, but an ab. *obscura* Closs, in the same species, basking in the sun underneath his front gate, was less fortunate. It is figured on Plate 43, figs 3, 4 (*Aberrations of British Butterflies*: Plate 21, figs 3, 3a).

THIS account of Don's life and his collecting experiences would not be complete without further mention of his collecting partner and companion, Mark Middleton, and some of the contributions he has made over the years to their joint collection.

They first met at the home of Bob Watson in the early sixties. Mark was gardening there and Don was painting specimens from Bob's collection. Several months later, Mark turned up one afternoon at Don's for a chat and a cup of tea and to view his collection. Mark already collected moths, having been encouraged in this by his close neighbour, Peter Robinson, co-inventor with his brother Hugh of the Robinson Mercury Vapour Moth Trap. Don introduced Mark to butterflies and their friendship built up from there. For the next fourteen years Don was to be a regular visitor to Mark's home in Sandy Down, cycling over every Wednesday afternoon to play mah-jong with Mark's mother and her friends, staying for supper and returning home at midnight.

Sometimes Don would stay with Mark when his mother went on holiday abroad and it was on one of these occasions, in 1968, that Don's artistic skills were put to a somewhat unconventional use. Mark had been breeding the Small Tortoiseshell and some had escaped in the living-room. The emerging butterflies had fluttered at the window in their bid for freedom, covering the nearby wallpaper in red meconium. Anxious not to incur Mrs Middleton's wrath upon her return, Don cycled back home, returned with his paint-box and skilfully touched out the incriminating evidence.

When the opportunity arose in 1988, Mark sold his home and went to live with Don. Over the years Mark has added some remarkable aberrations to their joint collection and many of these have been included in this book. There are two other captures worthy of mention. In 1979, while working in his neighbour's garden, Mark spotted a perfect Peacock ab. *belisaria* Oberthür sunning itself on a wall and he rushed back home for his net, only to find the butterfly gone on his return. He waited anxiously and finally the attractions of a nearby buddleia proved irresistible and his patience was rewarded. In the glorious 'Painted Lady year' of 1996, he captured a magnificent Painted Lady ab. *ocellata* Rebel on the buddleia by the back door at Coridon.

At the end of June 1968, Don and Mark visited Buttermere Fell, in the Lake District, for the Small Mountain Ringlet, *Erebia epiphron mnemon* (Haworth), the English subspecies. In completing a series of this very variable butterfly Mark captured a fine female example of ab. *latefasciata* Dioszeghy, at Honister Pass (*South's British Butterflies*: Plate 35, fig. 3). Five years later, they travelled to Ben Lawers in Perthshire for the larger and more brightly coloured *scotica* Cooke, the Scottish subspecies of this butterfly. On arrival at the small visitors' centre there, they were greeted by a pleasant young warden who came over, shook hands and enquired as to their particular interest in natural history - so different from the treatment they usually encountered from his southern counterparts. Some months later Don sent him a framed painting that he had done specially, showing the various named aberrations of the Small Mountain Ringlet, together with a short note explaining it was our only alpine species. He also included a copy of T. G. Howarth's *Colour Identification Guide to Butterflies of the British Isles*. Tony Pickles, visiting the area some time afterwards, was able to tell Don that he had seen the painting displayed at the centre on the wall behind the desk.

With two days of their Scottish holiday remaining, they decided to search for the Large Heath, *Coenonympha tullia scotica* Staudinger. A large colony was located around Loch Kinardochy and Don took three specimens of ab. *obsoleta* Tutt, with all the ocelli absent, having been told by one of his Yorkshire friends that no one had ever taken a complete *obsoleta* form.

Don and Mark spent several holidays in north-west Lancashire staying at either Arnside or the Derby Arms at Witherslack. On Arnside Knott, with its sweeping views over the Kent Estuary, they took ab. *infasciata* Warren in both colour forms in the Scotch Argus, *Erebia aethiops aethiops* (Esper) Plate 70, figs 1-4. Don was exceptionally fortunate to take in this species the bilateral gynandromorph figured on the same plate, figs 5, 6. He had boxed it, and being unable to determine its sex - one minute male, the next female - he did not consider it as being an aberration until it settled on the bottom of the pill-box, its wings open in the sun, its full qualities revealed. Cecil Haxby, who was with them at the time, came along and cautiously commented in his slow methodical style that it was '. . . certainly male on one side.' These three insects are also figured in *Aberrations of British Butterflies*: Plate 34, figs 8, 11, 13, 14.

Nearby Meathop Moss produced some spectacular ab. *lanceolata* Arkle of the Large Heath, *Coenonympha tullia davus* (Fabricius) for Don and Mark (*South's' British Butterflies*: Plate 43, figs 4, 7, and *Aberrations of British Butterflies*: Plate 40, figs 16-18). Tony Pickles and I joined them at their hotel, just below the Knott, for a rather wet week at the end of July, in 1972.

The Mendips in Somerset, were a favourite area for collecting in the 1970s. Visiting there with Don in 1974, I was fortunate enough to capture the magnificent male Dark Green Fritillary, Plate 53, figs 1, 2, as it fed at wild thyme with its black wings spread, in breathtaking contrast with the cushion of pink flowers. I remember running as fast as I could, stumbling over the rough ground, to show Don my wonderful prize. Earlier, in the mid-sixties at nearby Draycott, Don had worked a colony of Chalk Hill Blues in an uncultivated corner of a field. Having caught and released several males which appeared somewhat dull-looking, he eventually decided to keep four. When he came to set them he realised that they were approaching ab. *pulla* Bright & Leeds. There one day he met Norman Watkins who mentioned to Don taking a female Meadow Brown ab. *anticrassipuncta* Leeds at that locality (*South's British Butterflies*: Plate 39, fig. 7).

Enjoying a rest from a morning's collecting. Left to right: Ian Farwell, Don, Mark and myself. The flowery bank that once provided shelter and sustenance for the Chalk Hill Blue and other species has long since been obliterated by quarrying. Portland, Dorset, late 1970s.

I N 1971 Don introduced me to Portland, in Dorset. This rugged limestone promontory, with its commanding views, rich flora and insect life, has always possessed a magical quality for me. Collecting along the cliff tops in summer under clear blue skies with the Humming-bird Hawk-moth, *Macroglossum stellatarum* (L.) hovering over the pink valerian, often in the company of Clouded Yellows, Painted Ladies or the Red Admiral, *Vanessa atalanta* (L.), there is a special atmosphere to the place reminiscent of more southerly climes. Ever present, too, is the strong expectation that some really good migrant just might choose to make first landfall here in this favoured part of Wessex. Twenty years later, in September 1991, this expectation was to be personally fulfilled when I discovered Berger's Clouded Yellow, *Colias alfacariensis* Berger to be breeding at the High Angle Battery, near the Verne (Harmer, 1992).

Thus, Portland established itself as a favourite hunting ground for us all during the 1970s and early 1980s. At that time quarrying activity was minimal; road improvements, development, municipal landscaping and an increase in tourism had yet to take place. It possessed a wild freedom rarely encountered elsewhere on the South Coast and one could roam widely among the sheltered flowery banks and hollows to collect undisturbed. Although the Chalk Hill Blue was the main objective, there was always the possibility of something of interest turning up in the Silver-studded Blue, Small Copper, *Lycaena phlaeas eleus* (Fabricius), Meadow Brown, or the Grayling, providing an unexpected bonus. The Chalk Hill Blue was in fantastic numbers and 1975 and 1976 were especially great years. In the glorious summer of 1975, at Portland, Don captured a female Chalk Hill Blue ab. *ultraradiata* Bright & Leeds, a female Grayling ab. *monocellata* Lempke (*Aberrations of British Butterflies*: Plate 11, fig. 10; Plate 36, figs 4, 4a) and two female Chalk Hill Blue ab. *inaequalis* Tutt - all in a single morning! After celebrating with two ice-creams he set off for home to avoid carrying the prizes around any longer. On arrival home, the thermometer on the wall next to his front door had registered 95°F in the shade. At Portland in 1976, Mark caught the Small Skipper, *Thymelicus sylvestris* (Poda) ab. *pallida* Tutt, figured on Plate 1, figs 2, 2a, in *Aberrations of British Butterflies*. Many of the splendid aberrations taken by Don and Mark in those seasons were subsequently featured in two articles Don wrote for *The Entomologist's Record and Journal of Variation* (Russwurm, 1976 a and b).

I have lost count of the number of trips we made down to Portland in my Rover 2000 T.C. and if for any reason I was unable to accompany them, Don and Mark would travel by train to Weymouth, then take a bus or taxi out to Portland Heights. They stayed several times at the Royal Portland Arms in Fortuneswell where I joined them in 1975, for a few days collecting.

I have a particularly fond memory around this time, involving one of those coincidences in life. In early June 1976, my future wife Maggie and I were returning from Cornwall and, wanting a few Wood Whites for breeding, we decided to stop off at Branscombe, Devon, for a few hours. It was a fine, warm sunny day and after I had finished collecting I joined her for refreshments at the café on the beach. I remember sitting back, taking in the beautiful scenery and weather, and for some reason thinking to myself that it was a pity Don was not also there to enjoy it all. Immediately, as if on cue, two figures came ambling along the beach as I sat there in amazement. One of them was Don! With him was a friend from Bursledon, who was keen to take his own short series of the Wood White. They had come down that morning but had only managed to catch a few males. I was able to lead them to a spot along the base of the cliff where collecting was easier and where I had earlier found some females.

Throughout the 1970s and early 1980s one of our first trips of the season would be catching the Lymington ferry to Yarmouth, Isle of Wight in search of larvae of the Glanville Fritillary, *Melitaea cinxia* (L.). The black, spiky caterpillars with their dull-red heads were easily found as they fed in large groups on the plantain growing amongst the turf on the sandy undercliff. Mark bred out a number of the lovely underside form ab. *wittei* Geest (*Aberrations of British Butterflies*: Plate 30, figs 3, 3a). Don bred the ab. *expuncta* Cabeau figured on Plate 64, figs 5, 6. Their friend Ian Farwell had had earlier success with this species, particularly with melanic aberrations including ab. *horvathi* Aigner. His striking insects have been illustrated in *South's British Butterflies*: Plate 31, fig. 18; *Aberrations of British Butterflies*: Plate 30, figs 1, 1a; and here on Plate 64, figs 1-4.

A day out to the Isle of Wight.
Left to right: Andy Middleton, Steve Pittis, myself, Don, Mark, and John Scanes. April 1984.

Don's first recollection of Ian, in 1932, was of a young boy playing with the children of the family who ran the Old Tea House, opposite the Rose and Crown in Brockenhurst. (Don was on holiday at the time and his first Silver-washed Fritillary form *valesina* Esper was taken that year in Queen's Bower, opposite the Balmer Lawn). Ian lived at Portmore, just outside Lymington, for most of his life. Over the years he and his father had collected extensively in the New Forest, taking many of the Forest specialities and some of these captures have been included here. One of two bilateral gynandromorphs in the Silver-washed Fritillary taken by Ian, within a week of each other in Pignal Inclosure in 1939, is figured on Plate 60, fig. 3. In 1991 this specimen was on sale at Worldwide Butterflies for £120.

ONE particular collecting trip neither Don, Mark nor I will forget was in 1978. Having hired a Bedford Dormobile for a short holiday in Shropshire and North Wales at the end of June, we arrived at Whixall Moss in overcast and windy conditions. After a brief unsuccessful search for the Large Heath, Don and Mark, perhaps wisely, sought the safety and comfort of the vehicle, while I resolutely managed to put up a few specimens by quartering the boggy and uneven ground. Don, in any case, had by now become completely absorbed in the magnificent Small Tortoiseshell aberrations that were beginning to emerge from his temperature experiments; in many ways these were to be the highlight of the holiday.

We pushed on to Great Orme's Head, near Llandudno, arriving in the early evening just as the sea mist was closing in. I managed to convince them that this should not pose an obstacle to collecting, such would be the abundance of the dwarf race subspecies *caernensis* Thompson of the Silver-studded Blue. Mark and I set off, climbing up and along the slopes, while Don kept to the road. Our optimism was rewarded and we quickly took our series and made our way back to the van. By now the mist had worsened and visibility was down to a few yards. Don was even less visible, and in fact, was nowhere to be seen. Anxiously we drove slowly along the winding cliff road until his familiar figure eventually loomed up out of the mist, much to our relief. For his part he seemed completely unconcerned, having taken with the minimum of effort all the specimens he needed as they roosted upon the roadside vegetation. An uncomfortable night was then spent in Synchant Pass, being rocked to sleep by gale-force winds and horizontal rain.

THIS collection of happy memories could not finish without mentioning the marvellous 'Clouded Yellow year' of 1983, the best since 1947. In early August on the way back from Portland with Don, Mark, and John Scanes, we stopped off near Corfe Castle to explore a lucerne field I had discovered at the bottom of Brenscombe Hill. Although late in the afternoon, Clouded Yellows were still on the wing and Don netted a female to take home for closer examination. Later that evening he discovered to his delight that he had taken a very good ab. *striata* Geest (page 30). This lovely insect was not only featured on the colour plate of the *Proceedings and Transactions of The British Entomological and Natural History Society* the following year, but also on the front cover; a fitting reminder of an extraordinary season. It is comforting to know that such migrations, once a familiar sight to collectors of Don's generation, can still occur today. The extraordinary abundance of Painted Ladies in 1996 helped to reinforce that knowledge.

Regrettably, increasing osteoarthritis in his left hip eventually took over, and one day while collecting at Portland Don had to sit down as he was unable to go any further. He decided then it was perhaps finally time to hang up his net.

Reluctantly accepting his incapacity, and encouraged by his friend Karl Bailey's success, he turned his attention for the next few years to experimenting with temperature effect on pupae. He put a lot of effort into this, often having to get up at all hours of the night, leaving a nice warm bed to ensure that his pupae were getting the correct critical exposure to either heat or cold. His dedication was rewarded, however, with some wonderful aberrations of the Peacock, Small Tortoiseshell, Large Tortoiseshell and the Red Admiral.

Hod Hill, Dorset, June 1971.

Arnside Knott, Westmorland. '. . . with its sweeping views over the Kent Estuary.' August 1972.
Photo: Tony Pickles and reproduced by kind permission.

Don and Mark, Portland, Dorset, July 1975.

'Obligingly, Don pulled out a drawer from his cabinet and showed him the butterflies: five ab. *obliterae* in immaculate condition.' The plate of birds' eggs he painted for *Bird and Butterfly Mysteries* is in the background. Brockenhurst, December 1981.

Mark and Don looking at a drawer of Chalk Hill Blues from their joint collection. April 1999.

The unforgettable 'Clouded Yellow summer' of 1983. The lucerne field where Don took his female Clouded Yellow, *C. croceus* (Geoffroy) ab. *striata Geest* (see below). Corfe, Dorset, August 1983.

A new aberration of the Clouded Yellow, *C. croceus* (Geoffroy): ab. *russwurmi* Harmer - males (A. S. Harmer Collection). Photo: David Wilson and reproduced by kind permission.

Clouded Yellow, *C. croceus* (Geoffroy) ab. *striata Geest* - female (A. D. A. Russwurm Collection).

The Grayling, *Hipparchia semele semele* (L.) population on Portland displays a considerable range of development with regard to size and number of wing spots. Portland, Dorset, August 1987.

1996: the 'Painted Lady year'. They arrived in early June and were in unprecedented numbers by August. They nectared on the buddleias in their hundreds in the quarries on Portland before migrating southwards a few days later. Portland, Dorset, 16th August 1996.

The British Entomological and Natural History Society's Annual Exhibition at Chelsea Old Town Hall, London, 1st October 1986 - the final exhibition to be held there. Don joined the South London Entomological and Natural History Society (as it was then known) in 1952.
Left to right: Tony Pickles, Mark, Don, and Richard Revels.

Don, and Les Young. The Lycaenidae were particular favourites of Les and he will be especially remembered for his work with the Small Copper and the Common Blue. His collection was rich in the most marvellous aberrations in this family. Church Crookham, Hampshire, March 1991.

Don's 90th birthday party. Karl Bailey (left) looks on as Don, Mark, Ian Farwell and Steve Pittis admire the results of his temperature experiments. 'Karl's beastly fakes', as Don affectionately calls them. Lymington, Hampshire, June 1994.

Don cutting into the cake at his 90th birthday party, watched by Maggie Harmer. The cake was decorated with Clouded Yellows and Chalk Hill Blues. Lymington, Hampshire, June 1994.

95 not out! Celebrating at Coridon,
Brockenhurst, 11th June 1999.

Don's 95th birthday. Left to right: Graham Howarth, myself, Don, Tony Pickles and Mark. Coridon,
Brockenhurst, 11th June 1999.

Chapter Three

'A Cabinet of Rarities'

ONE CHRISTMAS morning, during the First World War, a boy waited with polite impatience while his parents tried to remember where they had hidden their son's present. 'It's in the wardrobe,' he desperately wanted to tell them but dared not. Of course he had known of its whereabouts for some time, having paid many a secret visit to the hiding place. Taking the present out, he would look at it avidly before carefully returning it once more, all the time hoping Christmas would jolly well hurry up. Well now, here it was at last and they could not remember! Eventually all was happily resolved and the boy was united with his present, a book entitled *The Butterflies of the British Isles* by Richard South. As the young lad studied the beautiful colour illustrations it contained in deep admiration, he could not have foreseen that in fifty years time he would be painting the plates for the updated revision of that original classic work: the new *South's British Butterflies*.

The ability to draw and paint seems to be hereditary in the Russwurm family. Don was about fourteen or fifteen years old when his father, an accomplished landscape artist, steered his son through the techniques of watercolour painting. He remembers that his father was helping him with his first attempt - a small harbour scene with some fishing boats - when his mother came into the room, 'Don't disturb him,' his father said, 'he's making rather a good job of this.'

Sadly, his father never saw any of his son's butterfly paintings as he died in 1952 at the age of seventy-four. It was to be another of Don's regrets that his mother, Ethel Violet, did not live to see the publication of *South's British Butterflies*. She had been thrilled by the proofs of the colour plates and had a stool by the side of her bed in readiness for the book. She died at the age of ninety and Don dedicated his *Aberrations of British Butterflies* to her memory. Happily his sister Anne has been able to enjoy his success. She, too, is an artist, specializing in ships of the Royal Navy, and has received many commissions and on several occasions has had her work hung in the Royal Academy.

Apart from his father's tuition, Don remained completely self-taught and he continued with his painting, mostly of landscape subjects, and working in oils. Whilst at the Eastern Telegraph Company he entered his efforts in the private art exhibitions sponsored by the chairman, Sir Edward Wilshaw. One year Don asked him if he would accept a painting of Porthcurno in Cornwall, where the transatlantic cables came ashore and the Company's station was situated. He was ushered into the boardroom to present the picture personally to Sir Edward and they chatted for quite a while. Sir Edward was delighted because of the many associations Porthcurno held for the Company and the picture was graciously received.

His work had also come to the attention of one of the staff, a Colonel Wellingham, who happened to know that Staples Press Ltd. were looking for an artist to illustrate a fortnightly magazine called *Nature Lover*. This was to be the start of Don's long and successful career as a butterfly artist.

H E BEGAN contributing articles to the magazine in 1948 with a review of his season's collecting accompanied by black and white illustrations depicting the species mentioned. Reviews for the 1949 and 1950 seasons were followed by an article entitled *Variation in Butterflies*, and featured eight aberrations. He had almost completed describing and illustrating the life histories of all the British species when the magazine ceased publication at the beginning of the 1950s. Friends were convinced that he had killed off the magazine, a fact not borne out by the publishers - according to Don!

About the same time that his work for *Nature Lover* began he illustrated *Butterfly Miracles and Mysteries*, by Captain Bernard Acworth, which was published in 1947.

Don went to stay with Acworth for a long weekend to discuss the book, and being aware that Acworth was well-known for his outrageous theories and for 'hotly contesting irrefutable facts', he sought his assurance that his reputation would not be compromised in any way by his association with the book. The book contained one colour plate together with pen and black ink drawings of each species and some additional early stages. After reading it one can fully appreciate Don's reservations. Later, he painted a plate of birds' eggs for Acworth's *Bird and Butterfly Mysteries*, published in 1955.

After the war, Don's interest in aberrations continued to grow steadily. In the 1950s he was living at Sanderstead in Surrey, close to his friends Roy Stockley and Ewart Bolton. When he was shown Stockley's magnificent female Chalk Hill Blue aberration (Plate 24, fig. 7) he asked if he might paint it; permission was given, with careful instructions to look after it.

F OLLOWING his retirement to the New Forest, Don had access to several local collections rich in aberrations. In 1962 together with Ian Farwell he went to visit John Turner in Bournemouth. A butcher by trade, he was a shy, retiring man and Don was one of the first to see his collection. Turner had been able to collect throughout the years of the war and had had first refusal of the Reverend John Marcon's captures, as well as having acquired some of the specimens from the collection of S. G. Castle Russell. He generously placed his fine collection at Don's disposal to select and paint anything he chose. Later on, accepting a commission from Marcon, Don painted all his aberrations for him, recalling that it turned out to be a very genial and friendly association.

H. J. Turner, Hod Hill, Dorset, 1950. Many of the aberrations featured in *South's British Butterflies* and in this book were from John Turner's collection. Photo: I. G. Farwell. (By kind permission of Hazel Farwell.)

Don steadily worked at developing his technique. Asked to describe how he manages to produce such beautiful life-like paintings, he says that he considers it vital to begin by achieving a perfect wing shape, paying maximum attention to the apical area. Perfect accuracy is demanded otherwise the slightest error will make it look misshapen. All this is done by eye, with a final check being carried out, if necessary, using a carefully placed mirror to highlight any flaws or irregularities in the drawing. Next, the neuration is added and the wing markings pencilled in. Using Winsor and Newton Artists' Water Colour, a ground colour wash is applied, followed by the general patterning, and then, gradually and carefully, the colours are built up. Great attention has to be paid to the colouring as it is very often the subject of the description. Finally, by the careful use of shading placed to the side of the specimen, a three-dimensional effect is achieved, appearing to lift the butterfly off the page.

His close attention to detail comes as a result of knowing his subjects intimately. For example, the characteristic antennae of the Lycaenids and large Nymphalids are faithfully reproduced by the use of delicate, fine, white cross-strokes. When Don was working on *South's British Butterflies*, Leslie Goodson asked him how he managed to achieve the silver on the underside of the Silver-washed Fritillary. Don replied that it was in his mind's eye and that if one was an artist it was possible to convey the same effect on to paper without spending too much time analysing how.

On average, a plate would take Don three days to complete, excluding any finishing touches that might be required. The Purple Emperor is one of his favourite subjects for painting and his skill is such that the ones figured on Plate 15 in *Aberrations of British Butterflies* were completed during one afternoon, in just four hours.

As Don's paintings of aberrations steadily increased in number, Ian Farwell suggested keeping them in loose-leaf albums, into which more pages could be incorporated as required. Initially done for his own amusement, interest in his work grew so much amongst his friends that, in addition to his own volumes, he also produced copies for John Turner, Robert Watson and Leonard Lloyd.

ONE DAY in 1966, on his way to visit his brother in Southampton, Richard Ford, of Watkins & Doncaster, dropped in on Don to deliver a moth trap. Looking at some paintings Don had done of his White Admiral aberrations, he enquired as to the condition of the actual specimens, remarking that so often they were in tatters. Obligingly, Don pulled out a drawer from his cabinet and showed him the butterflies - five ab. *obliterae* Robson & Gardner in immaculate condition. After examining more of Don's work, he turned to him and made the historic comment: 'You must do the plates for the new South!' This referred to the proposed revision of *The Butterflies of the British Isles* by Richard South, which had first appeared in 1906. He promised Don that he would speak to the publishers Frederick Warne & Co. Ltd.

Another artist was also being considered for the job and months passed without Don hearing anything. One morning, while returning from shopping in Brockenhurst, he suffered a nasty tumble when a lorry driver carelessly flung open his door, knocking Don off his bicycle. By the time he got home he was feeling pretty fed up. Waiting for him on the mat was a letter from Frederick Warne confirming that he had the job. To the aches and pains of his accident was added a feeling of panic at the enormity of the task ahead of him. As soon as work commenced, however, any concern he may have had quickly disappeared.

Some of Don's first paintings of aberrations appeared in *Nature Lover*, circa 1950.

From *Nature Lover*, circa 1950.

Richard Ford also sought his advice on how best to depict the early life-stages in the book and Don suggested that they should be painted. Warne initially offered that job to him as well, but, anxious not to overload Don, they later employed the services of another artist, Mr R. B. Davis. Later, when the two of them met, he told Don that his only fear was that his work would not match the high quality of Don's. However, as soon as Don, and Graham Howarth the book's author, saw the first drawings by Mr Davis there could be no doubt regarding his skill at copying Frohawk's early life stages.

The paintings took eighteen months to complete, for which Don received a fee of £350 plus £50 expenses. Four long-weekend visits were made to the Department of Entomology at Tring Museum, where the National Collection was housed, for Leslie Goodson to name the aberrations. The Collection was later moved to South Kensington, and Don completed the paintings there.

A large number of the specimens figured in 'South's' were from the Turner and Bessemer collections. Douglas Bessemer was a 'cheque-book' collector, buying on the advice of Mr L. Hugh Newman, and over the years had built up a wonderful collection. He died shortly before Don started work on the plates and Graham Howarth, on behalf of the Museum, arranged that his collection should remain at Lyndhurst until all the aberrations selected for inclusion had been completed. Mrs Bessemer asked Don if he would paint a dozen of the specimens she had especially bid for at auction on her husband's behalf and to which she had a strong attachment. Don generously obliged, painting them on a large panel which she hung on the wall at the end of her bed so that she might see them every morning when she woke up.

IT WAS to be a further five years before *South's British Butterflies* by T. G. Howarth was finally published in 1973, the delay due, apparently, to the difficulty in finding a printing process for the colour plates that would be acceptable both to the artist and the publisher. The *Colour Identification Guide to Butterflies of the British Isles* was published later that year, and reprinted in 1974. With an abridged text in tabular form it was, according to E. W. Classey, one of the reviewers, '. . . most interesting and readable in this form.' The lower price also brought it within range of the younger entomologist's pocket.

For reasons to do with the printing process, Don was originally given the choice of painting the butterflies one and a quarter or one and a half times life-size, with the intention that they would be reduced to natural size in the book. This did not turn out to be the case, despite Howarth's best efforts to persuade the publishers not to print them one and a quarter times life-size. It was only when the revised edition of the 'Colour Guide' was published in late 1984 that the opportunity was taken to print them as originally intended. In June that year, at a surprise party held at Ramley House, Pennington, in honour of his eightieth birthday, Don was presented with a proof copy of the revised plates. With his love of classical music the venue was quite fitting, being the former home of Sir Thomas Beecham whose concerts Don had attended many years earlier while living in Surrey.

These plates were used once more when the popular *Observers Butterflies* was revised in 1989. Much to Don's annoyance, the publishers, Penguin Group, wrongly stated that he had copied Frohawk's work. When the mistake was brought to their attention, they apologized, explaining that the error had arisen from insufficient information having been passed to them by Frederick Warne. They promised to correct the error in the next reprint. A glance at the work of these two artists will show their approach to the subject to be quite different. It is perhaps worth recording that owing to the terms of his original contract with Warne, Don never received any royalties for the reproduction of his work.

Don's paintings frequently appeared in various entomological journals. These included a series of spectacular aberrations of the Cinnabar, *Tyria jacobaeae* (L.), bred by R. W. Watson, his own Scotch Argus ab. *infasciata* Warren forms and a male Clouded Buff, *Diacrisia sannio* (L.) ab. *russwurmi* Watson. He had taken it at Fritham in July 1960, while collecting with Bob Watson. Bessemer, having heard of this capture, wanted to buy the insect but Bob was also interested and asked Don if it had been sold. Upon being told it had not, Bob promptly handed him two ten pound notes - a considerable sum in those days - and clinched the deal.

In 1969, Don was requested by Norman Riley on behalf of the Society for the Promotion of Nature Reserves to design a Christmas card. He donated a delightful picture of Large Blues. The following year the picture was used again, this time in the format of a telephone notepad.

IN 1976, when I first considered having the paintings in this book professionally bound, I loaned one of the volumes to a friend to show to a contact in the bookbinding business, who was so impressed by them that he wanted to publish them as a collector's item. It was explained that they were not really suitable for publication as they were. He in turn, however, passed them on to the Natural History Museum and they contacted Don in October that year to discuss possible publication, stating that they were sure the paintings would have enormous appeal.

In November I accompanied Don on his second trip to the Museum, to meet John Abraham, Senior Publications Officer, for further discussions. The intention was to publish a book containing forty plates of aberrations and, if successful, to follow it up with a second volume. I note from my diary that neither Don nor I were happy with this proposal as he had already written telling them that he thought at least fifty plates would be necessary. Their reason given later for restricting it to forty plates was that any additional plates would result in a disproportionate increase in costs.

Although approval had still to be obtained, it was generally understood that there would not be any problems. I recall that the meeting was brief and slightly vague and that issues such as layout were not discussed. My volume was returned and Don gave them the plates he had already done. Afterwards we went to the Department of Entomology and Don set to, painting some of the Reverend John Marcon's aberrations in the National Collection. Meanwhile, I busied myself going through the collection selecting specimens for Don's approval for inclusion in the book.

Work on the book was well under way when for some reason - possibly due to priority having to be given to publishing their own scientific research - the Museum decided not to proceed and called off the project. They did, however, advise Don that the publisher Eric Classey, who was already familiar with his work, had asked for permission to publish it himself and strongly advised Don to take up the offer. Although initially disappointed, he was pleased that it was going to be taken up by a publisher who also happened to be a skilled entomologist.

Classey came down the very next day to see him to discuss the book. Don was philosophical when Eric explained that he would be unable to offer him any payment for his efforts; Don saw it as being very much a labour of love - after all, he was not having to earn his living from it. (Later on, Eric Classey was able to make up for this in some measure by giving Don a generous number of complimentary copies of the book, including a handsome leather bound edition). He asked to see a sample of what Don had written so far and was handed the Introduction, which he read through in complete silence. Don's first reaction was 'Heavens! - is it really as bad as all that?' To his great relief, Classey told him that it was magnificent and urged Don to let him have it as soon as possible. He took the Introduction away with him together with one unfinished painting for use in the promotional colour brochure. He assured Don that the greatest care would be taken by the publishers and the printers and that nothing would appear without Don's approval.

And so in 1978, *Aberrations of British Butterflies* by A. D. A. Russwurm became a worthy successor to F. W. Frohawk's *Varieties of British Butterflies,* published in 1938, forty years earlier. Together, these two gentlemen share the distinction of being the only artists in this country that century to have written, illustrated and had published, books devoted entirely to the subject of aberrations.

Three and a half thousand copies of Don's book were printed and in it he featured specimens from the National Collection, his own collection and those of his many friends. In addition, it included many new aberrations taken since the completion of the plates for 'South's'. In particular, some of the splendid Silver-washed Fritillaries that were captured in Great Ridge, Wiltshire, during the unprecedented summer of 1976.

The book received excellent reviews. Don particularly remembers his initial reaction as being a sick feeling in the pit of his stomach when the first review arrived from Classey. It was from a German entomological journal in Frankfurt and ended: 'This beautiful book, itself a "cabinet of rarities", is warmly recommended to all specialists and connoisseurs of Lepidoptera. Great credit is due to the author as well as the publishers who so successfully promote the cause of Entomology.' Another German reviewer commented: 'All the butterflies look and give the impression of being real.'

English critics were no less generous in their praise. W. G. Tremewan writing in the *Entomologist's Gazette* stated: 'In producing this book the author is now firmly established as one of the foremost butterfly illustrators in Britain.' Michael Chalmers-Hunt, reviewing it for the *The Entomologist's Record and Journal of Variation,* said: 'We believe these illustrations the best that have yet appeared from this talented artist and have little doubt that the book will be well received.' Indeed, several of the reviewers remarked that in many ways his book was superior to Frohawk's, in terms of artistry, reproduction of the plates and arrangement of the figures.

S OME twenty years after its publication, *Aberrations of British Butterflies,* along with *South's British Butterflies,* has firmly established itself now as a classic, and deservedly so. For any serious work devoted to these most fascinating and beautiful of insects it has become an almost obligatory source of reference.

At the time Don was approached by Russell Bretherton of the British Entomological and Natural History Society about the possibility of a second volume, indicating that they might subscribe towards its publication. Don pointed out that Frohawk had stopped painting in his early seventies and that he, too, had now reached that age. Bretherton's immediate response was 'Oh! you're miles better than Frohawk.' High praise indeed. Nothing came of the offer, however, and instead Don busied himself by accepting several large commissions: all the British butterflies for Malcolm Simpson and a selection of moths and butterflies - including a few aberrations - for the Reverend Steve Pittis.

Over the last few years he has had to limit his painting output as, quite naturally, his eyesight is not as good as it used to be. He has concentrated mainly on producing his own entomological Christmas cards for his close friends. These are eagerly awaited and treasured by all.

Now, at the grand old age of ninety-five, Don is still painting despite proclaiming many times his intention to give it up!

Don working on his Grayling Christmas card. October 1994.

Some of the illustrations that accompanied Don's articles for *Nature Lover* on the life histories of butterflies, circa 1950. Photo: Printwise of Lymington and reproduced by kind permission.

From *Nature Lover*. The early life histories are a little-known facet of Don's work. Photo: Printwise of Lymington and reproduced by kind permission.

Large Blue Butterfly by A. D. A. Russwurm.

This painting of *Large Blues on Wild Thyme* was published by the Society for the Promotion of Nature Reserves as a Christmas card in 1969. They subsequently used it again featured this time on the cover of a telephone notepad.
(By kind permission of the Royal Society for Nature Conservation.)

From the original watercolour drawing by
A. D. A. Russwurm

Aberrations of *Diacrisia sannio* Hübner.

1. ab. *russwurmi* Watson ♂.
2. ab. *immarginata* Niepelt ♂.
3. ab. *deleta* Delahaye ♂.
4. ab. *rubescens* Gerhardinger ♂.

From the original watercolour drawing by
A. D. A. Russwurm

New aberrations of *Callimorpha jacobææ* L.

1. ab. *coneyi* Watson.
2. ab. *intermedia* Watson.
3. ab. *nigrofimbriata* Watson.
4. typical specimen from the same brood.

Left: The Clouded Buff, *Diacrisia sannio* (L.) ab. *russwurmi* Watson. Male taken by Don at Fritham in the New Forest, in July 1960, and subsequently named after him. From *The Entomologist's Record and Journal of Variation*, Volume 87, October 1975. (By kind permission of the Editor, *The Entomologist's Record and Journal of Variation*.)

Right: The Cinnabar, *Tyria jacobaeae* (L.) This spectacular new aberration originated from a chance capture of a female by a Dorset schoolboy. She laid eggs in a jam jar before being released. From the *Proceedings and Transactions of The South London Entomological and Natural History Society*, August 1967, Part 3. (By kind permission of the Editor, British Entomological and Natural History Society.)

Ornithoptera on Fire-screen.

Don has brightened up several pieces around his home with paintings of Birdwing butterflies. The original specimens were obtained in exchange for his surplus *Chrysiridia croesus* Gerstaecker during the war. The Queen Alexandra's Birdwing, *Ornithoptera alexandrae* Rothschild (centre) bore the label of the famous collector A. S. Meek. Of particular significance to Don was the date of capture: 1904 - the year he was born. Photo: Printwise of Lymington and reproduced by kind permission.

Don with some of the books he has illustrated over the years: *South's British Butterflies; Colour Identification Guide to Butterflies of the British Isles;* and *Aberrations of British Butterflies.* Brockenhurst, December 1981.

Signing *'South's'.* Graham Howarth, author of *South's British Butterflies* and Don who illustrated the adult stages. Brockenhurst, November 1996.

Don Russwurm. His oil painting of Porthchapel near Land's End, Cornwall, is on the wall behind. January 1999.

Relaxing with a good book! On the wall behind Don are some of his paintings. Left to right: Corfe Castle, Dorset; Logan Rock near Porthcurno, Cornwall; Porthchapel near Land's End, Cornwall; and the Solent viewed from Boldre. The Camberwell Beauty is by Tim Bernhard. January 1999.

PART TWO:

Genetics and Variation, Breeding

Chapter Four

Butterfly Genetics: in Theory

Tʜʀᴏᴜɢʜᴏᴜᴛ the greater part of our long, rich collecting heritage spanning some three centuries or more, aberrations have attracted the curiosity and attention of British collectors. Our relative paucity of species when compared to the numbers enjoyed by European lepidopterists has been an instrumental factor in the huge interest and study these unusual forms have received in the past and continue to receive. Continental collectors have long regarded Britain as being exceptionally favoured with respect to the apparent abundance of aberrations. Possibly, the British Isles isolated geographically as they are, with a changeable maritime climate, provide conditions more conducive to producing these forms than on mainland Europe. Whatever the reasons may be, we are indeed extremely fortunate.

The sheer wealth of diversity displayed by the aberrations featured in this book invites contemplation and speculation on the possible reasons - forces and laws of nature even - which could account for their appearance. Indeed, such laws do exist. There is still a great deal not fully understood regarding the exact origins of these enigmatic anomalies of nature and about which we can only surmise - at least for the present. Perhaps this very lack of knowledge and the mystery that surrounds them adds to their appeal.

These remaining chapters aim to provide some of the pieces to the fascinating puzzle these aberrations present. Before doing so, we might begin by considering the usage of the terms 'variety', 'variation' and 'aberration' and the meanings that have been assigned to them in the literature over the years.

VARIATION AND ABERRATION

Iɴ *Natural History of British Butterflies*, published in 1924, Frohawk referred to what he considered was the misuse of the word 'varieties', which he remarked was often applied to geographical forms, subspecies and sexual dimorphic forms as well as to individual - often extreme - aberrations. He chose to confine the use of the word 'variety' to '... denote an aberration or a sport which differs from the normal type in some such detail as the pattern or the colour of the wings.' He included gynandromorphism within his definition. Later, in 1938, in *Varieties of British Butterflies*, he reaffirmed his earlier view, defining 'aberration' as being 'when a specimen varies in markings and coloration from geographical races and seasonal forms; differing from the normal type.' He added homoeosis to this definition. Accordingly, what had been var. *obsoleta* of the Large Blue in *Natural History of British Butterflies*, subsequently became ab. *obsoleta* in *Varieties of British Butterflies*.

In 1973, in *Colour Identification Guide to Butterflies of the British Isles*, Graham Howarth described 'variation' as an all-embracing term covering all aspects of difference, dividing some twenty forms of variation into two classes: individual and collective. The first class comprised abnormalities essentially of an individual nature, involving sexual, structural, and pathological phenomena, e.g. gynandromorphs, intersexes, somatic mosaics, homoeosis, peroneural and scale defects, and hybridization. The second class contained geographical races or subspecies, geologically associated forms, seasonal and sexual dimorphism, polymorphism, albinism and melanism (although in some moths, melanism is also associated with polymorphism) and, lastly, aberrations. For the most part, aberrations generally divide into two broad groups: those where the normal wing ground colour has been affected, and those where the extent - in either direction - of wing pattern or spot markings has been markedly altered.

As examples from both these classes have been featured in this book, it is appropriate that the word 'variation' should appear in the title, although aberrations will be the principal focus of our attention.

GENETICS

MANY READERS will already be familiar with E. B. Ford's *Butterflies*. Published in 1945, the first in the popular New Naturalist Series, it was a milestone in the history of butterfly literature. In this classic work, Professor Edmund Brisco Ford broke new ground by including several chapters dealing with theoretical genetics and their practical application to butterflies. His immense scientific knowledge enabled him to convey the complexities of heredity with a clarity of prose that made the subject both understandable and absorbing for his readers. Although there have been enormous advances in the field of genetics since *Butterflies* was first published, the principles of heredity which he wrote about are still valid today. Books devoted solely to the study of genetics in Lepidoptera are rare as most research work has been carried out in other Orders and, because of their specialist nature, do not remain in print very long. Fortunately, copies of *Butterflies* are still easily obtainable at reasonable prices. In addition, *Mendelism and Evolution*, and *Moths* by the same author, are excellent reference works.

To have attempted to emulate Ford's work here would have been going beyond the scope and indeed the original intention of this book. However, not to have explained the underlying genetics responsible for many of the aberrations so beautifully figured here would have been a wasted opportunity. Admittedly, the rarity and beauty of aberrations can be admired without any comprehension at all of genetics, but with just a little basic understanding of the subject, the principles involved and their practical application, this admiration can be appreciably enhanced. Ford inspired lepidopterists to learn more about the aberrations they encountered in the field, being keen to point out the new and exciting possibilities and rewards such knowledge could bring to the collector. As a consequence, some of the genetic examples about which he could only surmise have since been validated through breeding. In the half century since *Butterflies* there have been new discoveries, and numerous contributions published in the many entomological journals. This book has provided the ideal opportunity for consolidating some of these findings.

Those keen to follow Ford's advice should appreciate that successful results are by no means assured. Quite apart from the sub-viable nature of some of the genes responsible for aberrations, allied to the close lines of breeding required and the reluctance on the part of some species to pair in captivity, there are other factors such as weather, disease and predators to contend with. All these obstacles will seek to conspire against the breeder to ensure that from time to time, inevitably, frustration and disappointment will prevail. Finding ways to overcome these challenges is integral to the enjoyment and satisfaction this fascinating pursuit provides. There is, too, the opportunity to contribute to our existing knowledge through the publication of one's research. With this in mind, it is important that all breeding experiments are conducted methodically and that detailed notes be kept. Never rely solely on memory!

Genetics can be defined as the study of heredity and variation. Undoubtedly, it is an extremely complex subject and in view of this I have tried to confine its treatment here very much at a level which I consider other keen amateur lepidopterists like myself would not only find understandable, but also useful in pursuing their hobby. At best this can only be a relatively superficial introduction into this fascinating branch of science. Nevertheless, the information included should be sufficient to meet the needs and majority of circumstances the breeder is likely to encounter. For anyone wanting to learn more about genetics, the choice of medium for doing so has never been so broad. Modern school biology books at secondary education level adequately cover the subject and are packed with excellent graphics, illustrating and explaining every detail. Besides books and videos, there is the personal computer with Cd rom facility, and connection to the Internet allows access to World Wide Web addresses, providing a further rich and excellent source of information.

THE PRINCIPLES OF MENDELIAN INHERITANCE

BEFORE considering some of the different mechanisms whereby genetic information is passed on to subsequent generations, this would be an appropriate point to take a step back and to reflect upon the fact that quite a few of the aberrations featured in this book are governed by genetic principles originally worked out over one hundred and thirty five years ago by Father Gregor Mendel, Abbot of the Augustinian monastery of St. Thomas at Brünn, in what was formerly Moravia. For those readers who have only vague memories of Mendelism from their distant schooldays, or are otherwise unfamiliar with his work, a brief summary is given below. What is meant by Mendelian inheritance is explained, and its relevance to butterflies, and thus its importance to lepidopterists, will become apparent in due course. Inevitably, in discussing genetics, the use of technical terms is largely unavoidable and on their initial introduction these keywords appear in italics for convenience of identification and subsequent reference elsewhere.

Through the careful selection of the pea, *Pisum sativum,* as the subject for his experiments, Mendel was not only able to explain how heredity functioned, he also devised the method for carrying out such genetic experiments. He sought to discover the result when two plants differing in only one contrasting *character* or *feature* e.g. tall and dwarf for the character 'stem length' were combined to form a *monohybrid cross* (in this context, the word hybrid is used to describe the offspring of two different varieties as opposed to different species). He verified that all the characters were pure-breeding before studying them and, using self-pollination, continued his experiments through several generations.

From these experiments he discovered that in the *first filial generation* (*F₁*) all the plants were identical, resembling the tall parent in height. Only one of the contrasting characters - in this instance the character for tallness - had appeared and he described this as being the *dominant* form. The dwarf character did not appear and he called this the *recessive* form. He established from his experiments that it was immaterial which of the parents (or *P₁ generation*) contributed the different characters: the results were the same. Visually, the F_1 generation was identical to the tall parent which meant that Mendel was unable to confirm what he suspected: that each parent had been passed on their own qualitative character equally to every individual of the F_1 generation. He managed to overcome this difficulty by performing a simple experiment called a *test cross* which he achieved by pairing a long-stemmed F_1 hybrid with a short stemmed plant (which he had already established as being a pure-breeding recessive). The resulting progeny exhibited both characters in approximately equal frequency, confirming that the two characters had indeed segregated - or separated - independently of each other.

The plants of the F_1 generation were allowed to self-pollinate and the resulting seed produced the *second filial generation* (*F₂*). In this generation, the dwarf character reappeared, but in a ratio of 3 tall (dominant) : 1 dwarf (recessive).

To establish how the plants of the F_2 generation would breed, Mendel let them self-pollinate and from the seed produced went on to raise a *third filial generation* (*F₃*). He discovered that all the dwarf plants and a third of the tall plants were pure-breeding for their respective characters and the remaining two tall plants both produced a mixture of both characters in a ratio of 3 tall (dominant) : 1 dwarf (recessive). From these results he was able to establish that the 3 (dominant) : 1 (recessive) ratio he had noticed in the F_2 generation could be further separated into a 1 (pure-breeding dominant) : 2 (mixed breeding dominants) : 1 (pure-breeding recessive).

Altogether, Mendel repeated these experiments using six other pairs of contrasting characters and found that the results were similar. His research led him to conclude that characters did not blend together (a commonly held belief at the time) but instead remained distinct and later on separated quite cleanly. From this he reasoned that it could not be the character itself being passed on during reproduction but some *factor* or *cell element* which determined that character. Each parent had to possess two of these cell elements for any given character, but only one was present in the *sex cell* or *gamete*. In referring to cell elements and their behaviour, Mendel had, in fact, predicted the units of heredity we now call *genes*.

This work led to what has since been described as *'Mendel's First Law'* or *'The Law of Segregation'* namely: *The characteristics of an organism are determined by pairs of factors of which only one can be present in each gamete.* An example of this particular form of Mendelian inheritance, involving a monohybrid cross, is represented in Diagram 2.

Mendel then went on further to investigate the effects of combining two pairs of contrasting characters, e.g. stem height and petal colour, seed coat shape and colour etc. in the same hybrid i.e. a *dihybrid cross*. From his previous experiments he already knew which of these characters were dominant or recessive. In the F_1 generation the results were the same as had occurred in his monohybrid cross i.e. only the dominant characters appeared. In the F_2 generation he ended up with four different combinations of characters in a ratio of 9 : 3 : 3 : 1, of which two resembled the grandparents, whilst the other two combined together characters from both of the grandparents. Diagrams 4 and 5 explain the mode of transmission of genes in a dihybrid cross. Again, by test crossing, Mendel was able to confirm that the two characters segregated independently of each other. This was later defined as 'Mendel's Second Law' which is 'The Law of Independent Assortment' or 'The Law of Independent Segregation', namely: *When two or more pairs of characters are brought together in a cross they segregate independently of each other and may combine randomly with either of another pair.*

It should be mentioned that there are no definitive versions of these two laws and since their inception they have been re-defined to take into account modern discoveries. However, the original concepts are still valid.

What is particularly special about Mendel and his work is that he understood the mathematical significance of the ratios he achieved in his results. He used large numbers of plants in his experiments to confirm that these ratios were accurate. Starting his research in 1856, he published his findings on heredity ten years later. However, the importance of his work was not appreciated until the beginning of this century.

Over time, Mendel's results and conclusions have been substantiated through the tremendous amount of research into cell structure carried out since. His theories regarding cell elements and their behaviour are best explained by considering cells and the manner in which they reproduce themselves.

CELL STRUCTURE

B UTTERFLIES, in common with other organisms, are composed of large numbers of cells. With the exception of a few specialized cells, each cell essentially contains a *nucleus* and *cytoplasm*. Within the nucleus are a number of thread-like strands called *chromosomes*, on which are located structures known as genes that determine or code for the myriad different characters or features that constitute a species. This genetic material is made up of a chemical substance called DNA *(deoxyribonucleic acid)*, a large molecule consisting of two thin, long strands running parallel to each other in the form of a double helix, not unlike a spiral staircase.

Although chromosomes differ greatly both in shape and size, they are present in paired sets of two with each chromosome in the set having originated from one of the parents. These paired sets are identical in shape, size and for the genes that will code for the same characteristics e.g. ground colour, spot size etc. They are referred to as *homologous chromosomes* or *homologues*. The exception to this are the pair constituting the *sex-chromosomes* which are discussed further on. Those chromosomes not directly involved in determining sex are referred to as the *autosomes*. Each of the genes in a paired set occupies a specific position or *locus* on these chromosomes. Genes which determine the same character are located opposite each other on their respective chromosome and are called *allelomorphs* - or *alleles* for short (Diagram 1). Thus for any given character or trait, both homologous chromosomes will each carry a gene for that character. However, whilst the genes can be identical or *homozygous* i.e. giving identical instructions for the same characteristic (the individual being referred to as the *homozygote*), they may also be dissimilar or *heterozygous*, with the individual termed the *heterozygote*. For example, one gene may code for normal spot pattern, the other for elongated spotting. As Mendel discovered in his F_1 hybrids, the genetic make-up of an individual cannot always be determined by its physical appearance. When using the words homozygous and heterozygous we are in fact referring to the genetic constitution or *genotype* of the individual at a particular gene locus.

When the genotype is not known the term *phenotype* is applied to describe the actual physical appearance of the individual concerned. Phenotypes can be defined as 'the product of the interaction between an organism's genotype and its environment: the observable characters of an organism' (Majerus, 1994). Whereas physical appearance can be influenced environmentally, the genotype of the organism is not altered. Mendel's test cross technique can now be seen as the means whereby the genotype of an individual can be established simply by pairing it with another that is a homozygous recessive for the same character.

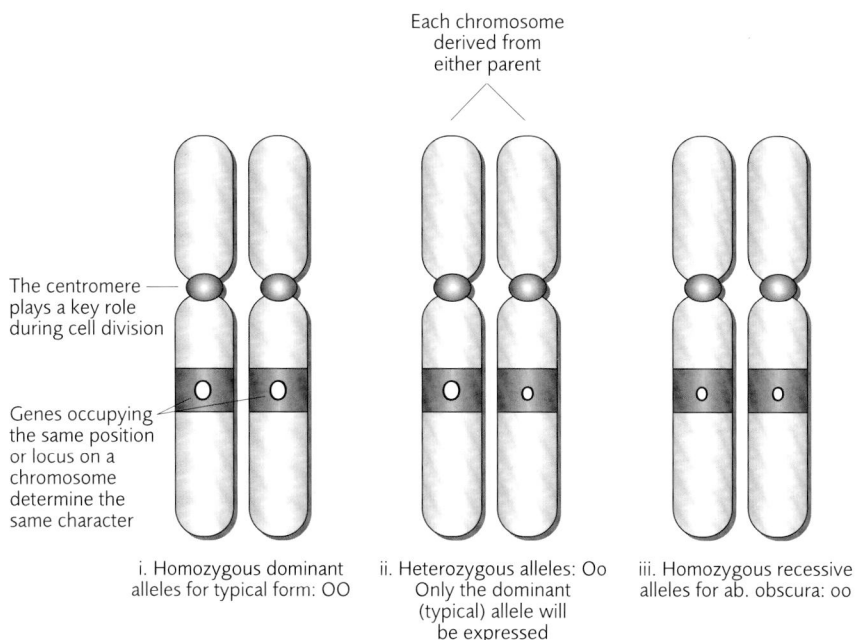

Each chromosome
derived from
either parent

The centromere
plays a key role
during cell division

Genes occupying
the same position
or locus on a
chromosome
determine the
same character

i. Homozygous dominant
alleles for typical form: OO

ii. Heterozygous alleles: Oo
Only the dominant
(typical) allele will
be expressed

iii. Homozygous recessive
alleles for ab. obscura: oo

DIAGRAM 1

THE RELATIONSHIP BETWEEN
GENES AND CHROMOSOMES

**The three different alleles present in a pairing between a typical Swallowtail,
Papilio machaon britannicus Seitz and ab. *obscura* Frohawk (see Diagram 2)**

With the exception of the gametes, the nucleus of most cells contains paired sets of chromosomes (homologues), each parent having contributed one chromosome to the pair. These homologous pairs of chromosomes determine or code for the same characters in the butterfly. Within any given pair, genes occupying corresponding positions or loci control the same character and are referred to as alleles. While the genes of an allelic pair determine a particular character, and may do so in an identical manner, one allele may control that expression differently. Alleles can be described as any of the alternative forms of a particular gene.

For simplification, other genes carried on the chromosomes have been omitted.

CELL TYPES AND CELL REPRODUCTION: MITOSIS AND MEIOSIS

Two cell types need to be considered in respect of their relevance to heredity, each having entirely different roles and methods of reproduction. The cells that constitute practically all the organs and various structures and tissues of the individual are called the *body cells* or *somatic cells*. The nucleus of each of these cells contains a full set of chromosomes carrying the genetic information for creating that organism - a 'blueprint for life' as it were. Vast numbers of these somatic cells are constantly being made either to facilitate growth or to replace damaged cells.

Somatic cells reproduce by a process of cell division known as *mitosis* in which each chromosome replicates itself, before dividing and separating, eventually to form two *daughter cells* from the original cell, each with an identical set of chromosomes. Occasionally, one of these cells may not receive an identical set of genetic information and the effect this can have on future development is discussed further on when considering gynandromorphism. Any mutation that may occur during mitotic division of somatic cells usually only affects that particular individual and cannot be passed on to its progeny. This is an important distinction between mitosis and the next method of cell reproduction to be described.

It was mentioned that somatic cells contain a full set of chromosomes (or what is referred to as the *diploid number*), each half of the set donated by each of the parents. As mitosis involves replicating full sets of chromosomes each time, it follows from what has been said that it can neither be the mechanism by which the somatic cells originally obtained their chromosome complement, nor that by which genes are passed on to the next generation. There needs to be a mechanism by which the chromosome number in a cell is halved (*haploid number*) in order to avoid a doubling of the chromosomal content of the cell. There is, and it is called *meiosis*.

Butterflies start life as a single cell or *zygote*, formed at the fusion or fertilisation of the female egg by the male sperm. Each of these gametes has a nucleus carrying half the genetic material i.e. chromosomes necessary for determining the similarities or differences of the potential offspring. This reduction of the chromosomal content in the gametes to the haploid number comes about through meiosis The fusion of the gametes restores the chromosomes to their full complement once more.

Meiosis is a special type of cell division peculiar to the production of the eggs and sperm i.e. the gametes or sex cells for the purpose of sexual reproduction. It involves two cycles of *cell division* or *cleavage* and it is the key to understanding the mechanism of heredity. It is essential therefore to have a clear understanding of the changes that occur to chromosomes and the genes they carry, during meiosis. Not only is meiosis unique to gamete production but, equally important, it provides the framework and opportunity for genetic variation and mutation to occur - so vital for a species in evolutionary terms.

The gametes are produced in the reproductive organs of the parents: the testes in the male and the ovaries in the female. For most of the time chromosomes exist as single threads randomly distributed within the cell nucleus. In readiness for meiosis, each chromosome starts to contract and thicken and to pair up with its homologous partner, before they produce copies of themselves (*sister chromatids*). These pairs of chromosomes are now quadruplet in appearance, each of the pair being referred to as a *bivalent*. The wall of the nucleus breaks down and the bivalents arrange themselves around the equator of the *spindle* (a barrel-shaped structure organized in the cytoplasm, composed of numerous *spindle fibres*) lying side by side, in intimate contact and attached to each other at one point by what is termed a *centromere*. In turn, the centromere is attached to the spindle.

One very pertinent observation needs to be made at this point because of its overwhelming importance in heredity and variation, and that is the totally random manner in which all the homologous pairs of chromosomes position and align themselves about the equator of the spindle in cell division. It is down to chance as to which side of the equator they may find themselves (Diagram 4). This randomness is not significant in mitosis as no pairing up of homologues occurs. In meiosis, however, when homologous chromosomes are present with alleles that code for alternative expressions of the same character, this random alignment allows new combinations of the genes on different chromosomes to occur. Sometimes, new combinations of characters can also arise at this stage through an exchange of equivalent portions or lengths of genetic material between homologous chromosomes (*recombination*). This process is termed *crossing over* and involves the breaking and rejoining of the chromatids. It does not automatically happen every time in meiosis and there is evidence that no recombination occurs in female Lepidoptera at meiosis (Robinson, 1971). As crossing over is not a factor in the basic genetic principles under discussion here, it need not be of further concern except to point out that its relevance to the breeder lies in its potential to produce new combinations of characters by splitting genes occurring on the same chromosome. It should be considered as one of several possible explanations when expected Mendelian ratios are not achieved.

Having arranged themselves either side of the cell's equator, the sister chromatids continue to contract and thicken to facilitate their eventual division. They are drawn apart to the opposite poles of the cell and this separation leads to the formation of two *intermediate cells*. The first division stage of meiosis is a reduction division which results in each of the intermediate cells containing only half of a set of chromosomes. In the second division that follows, the chromatids in these intermediate cells separate in mitotic fashion forming four daughter cells from the original cell, each with only half a set of chromosomes. These daughter cells are in fact the gametes.

The points discussed so far in this chapter can now be summarized as follows:
- genes are units of heredity that determine or control a particular character or feature, remaining always as discrete units and not blending with each other;
- when two or more pairs of characters are brought together in a cross they separate independently of each other and may come together in new combinations;
- genes are carried on the chromosomes in the nucleus of the cell. Chromosomes occur in paired sets i.e. homologues, with one chromosome being derived from each of the parents. Each chromosome in the pair is identical in shape and size and also for genes that will determine the same characters or features;
- each body cell contains two copies of each gene (one derived from each of the parents) determining or coding for the same character. These pairs of genes, known as alleles, are located opposite each other at the same locus or position as their respective homologous chromosome partner;
- the two genes that make up the alleles may be identical in the way they determine the expression of that character (homozygous) or they may code for different versions of the same character (heterozygous). One version of the gene may be dominant in its effect over the other;

- mitosis is a mechanism of cell reproduction whereby identical copies of genetic information are passed on to daughter cells during the growth and development of the organism;
- meiosis is necessary for halving the chromosomal content of the nucleus, essential for the formation of gametes during the process of sexual reproduction;
- during meiosis, homologous chromosomes segregate independently and randomly align themselves, giving rise to new genetic combinations;
- when gametes fuse to form the zygote, the full chromosome number is restored in the nucleus.

Although it is now known that genetics is a very much more complicated subject, Mendel's findings are still valid and remain the basis of inheritance. It is known, for example, that there are instances when neither gene present in an allele has complete dominance over the other. A single gene may, as Mendel was able to demonstrate, control the expression of just one character with no input from other genes. Alternatively, several genes may control the expression of a single character and sometimes several characters may be determined by a single gene. Some of these different aspects of heredity are discussed later on.

HOW ABERRATIONS ARISE

ABERRATIONS are the product of previous changes or mutations in the genetic make-up that determines the individual's physical appearance. Logically, it must have been gene mutation originally that provided the contrasting characters for any given feature. It is inevitable that during the constant and complex process of cell division scope for error does exist. In the process of the genetic material (DNA) replicating itself as a prelude to meiosis, portions may be partially or completely lost, inserted in the wrong position, possibly reversed, or even end up being incorrectly reattached. Such errors affect normal functional processes and occasionally result in character differences, producing a sudden and distinct departure from the normal or typical form. Surprisingly though, given the complexity of the operation, the frequency rate of mutation for a given gene is estimated as being extremely low, perhaps one individual in a million (Ford, 1945), although this frequency rate can be much higher, depending on the species and the particular genes involved. Most aberrations, however, arise through recombination of existing genes.

The consequences of gene mutation can be mixed. Sometimes the effect may be indiscernible or neutral, and not being under any selective pressure, the altered gene survives, to be carried in the population. Occasionally, mutation may prove beneficial for the species concerned; after all, the changes brought about by inherited variation are an essential part of evolution. More often though, the effect is to upset a gene's normal *modus operandi* to the extent that it becomes debilitating or even lethal for the organism concerned.

While in butterflies the effect of an aberrant gene is most observable in the imago through altered wing markings, it may in addition produce discernible effects in the earlier stages. For example, the pupa of the sombre-looking aberration, ab. *atratus* Bailey, in the Marsh Fritillary, is strikingly different in coloration from that of the normal form: the ground colour is pure white and the normal yellow markings are replaced by blackish maroon (Bailey, 1998).

Similarly, the same mutant gene may very well determine other less obvious functions which in their homozygous state frequently have a debilitating - even lethal

- effect on all stages of development, causing poor fertility rates in ova, failure in hatching and inexplicable larval losses - all signs of *inbreeding depression*. After inbreeding ab. *lanceolata* Shipp in the Ringlet for several generations, I found that out of a total of 276 ova resulting from several F_4 pairings, 129 ova proved infertile and 95 ova failed to hatch. By recording such losses any possible differential mortality of genotypes, particularly amongst homozygotes, can be examined.

All these points need to be kept in mind when attempting to interpret results deviating from expected Mendelian ratios. Whilst these ratios are constant over a large sample size, nevertheless they remain subject to the laws of chance, so a possible element of bias is introduced on the occasions when only a relatively small amount of material is available for analysis. In such instances, to establish whether or not the extent of deviation between the observed and expected ratios is significant or not there are statistical methods - the *chi-squared test* and *chi-squared table* - which can be employed. These enable the probability of chance alone accounting for the deviation to be determined. The reader will need to have recourse to a genetics textbook for an authoritative explanation of their application and interpretation.

Deciding whether or not a mutation is heritable and, if it is, how the necessary transmission is accomplished, is the subject of these remaining chapters. What knowledge we do have about the genetics of our butterflies is largely through the efforts of amateur lepidopterists. Since Ford's *Butterflies*, we now know that female *sex-linked inheritance* occurs in British butterflies (page 80), and there remains the possibility that other genetic phenomena such as *multiple allelomorphism*, (where a gene is determined by more than two alleles), male *sex linkage* etc. may yet be discovered in British butterflies. However, the existence of these phenomena in other species does not automatically mean that they must occur also in butterflies. Even in moths there are several instances of genetic interaction not mirrored in our butterflies; the polymorphic forms of melanism immediately come to mind. Such future discoveries will rely on the breeder's ability to observe closely and interpret the results of his research. Further on, in instances where our understanding of the genetics involved is either lacking or incomplete, I have expressed my own view, fully aware of the inherent dangers in doing so. Doubtless, over the course of time such opinions will be validated or proved incorrect. If nothing else, these gaps in our knowledge are an indication of how comparatively little we do know about even some of our more common aberrations. I rather hope that collectors will think of this as something of a challenge.

Having explained the basic principles of inheritance we can now go on to consider the various genetic mechanisms by which aberrations arise. In doing so, the relevance and application of Mendelism will become increasingly apparent.

MONOHYBRID INHERITANCE:
RECESSIVE GENES (SINGLE GENE DIFFERENCE)

To REPEAT what was said earlier, an individual carrying identical alleles for any given character is described as being homozygous for that character, and the individual, the homozygote. Such genes can be either dominant or recessive in their expression. In butterflies, aberrations controlled by dominant - as opposed to recessive - genes are encountered far more rarely, partly due to the fact that it would be an extremely rare event for both genes constituting the alleles (each on their respective chromosomes) to be affected simultaneously by mutation. The unaltered gene in the pair would in all probability be coding for the normal dominant

typical male   ab. *obscura* female

Parents (P₁) generation   O O   x   o o

alleles segregate to form gametes by meiosis.
each parent produces only one kind of gamete

Gametes produced by parents   O   o

gametes fuse to form zygote

First filial (F₁) generation   typical O o   x   O o typical

segregation by meiosis   segregation by meiosis

Gametes produced by F₁ generation   O   o   O   o

Gametes combined randomly in pairs

Second filial (F₂) generation   O O   O o   O o   o o

typical homozygous   typical heterozygous   typical heterozygous   ab. *obscura* homozygous

DIAGRAM 2

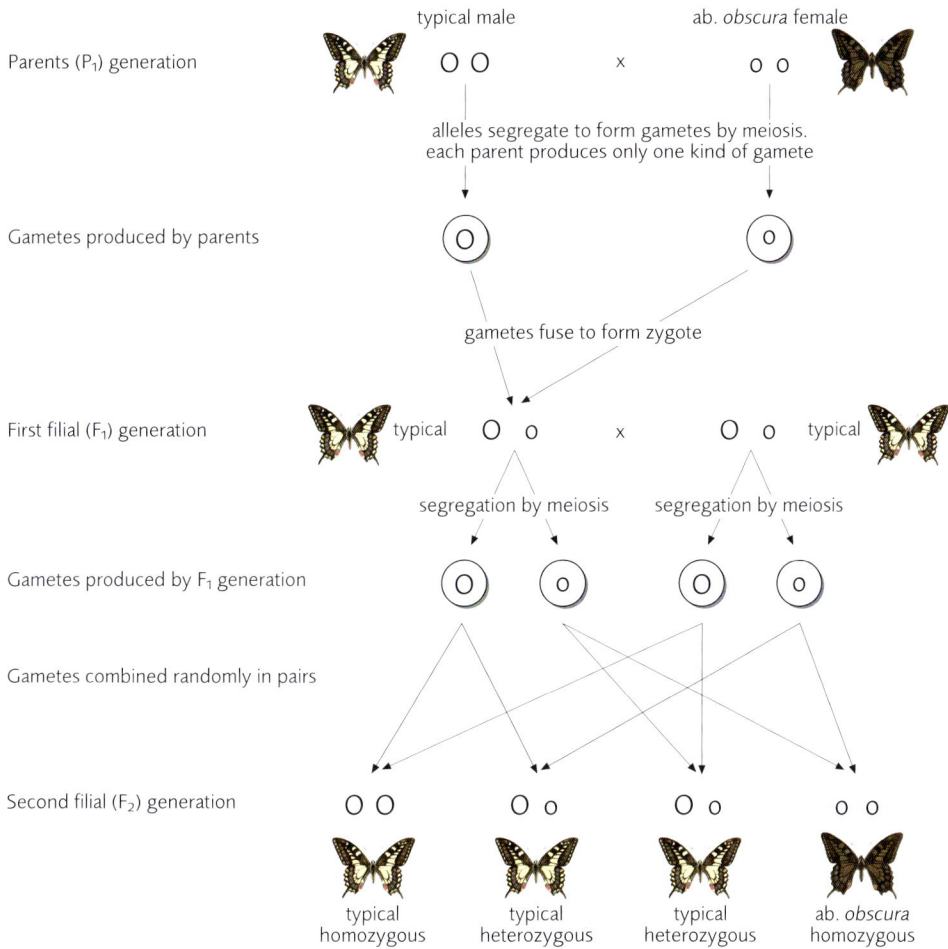

MONOHYBRID INHERITANCE:
SINGLE RECESSIVE GENE DIFFERENCE

Mode of transmission of the recessive allele for ab. *obscura* Frohawk in the Swallowtail, *Papilio machaon britannicus* Seitz

Homologous pairs of chromosomes pair up in meiosis (gamete formation). They carry pairs of genes (alleles) that control the same character. The alleles segregate, with each parent producing only one kind of gamete. All the heterozygous F₁ generation are typical. In the F₂ generation the expected Mendelian ratio for a monohybrid cross i.e. 3 (typical) : 1 (ab. *obscura*) should appear.

The diagram demonstrates Mendel's Law of Segregation i.e. contrasting forms of a character are determined by pairs of unlike alleles which separate into the different gametes. Only one gene of the pair can be present in each gamete.

expression of that character in the natural state and as such it would maintain this expression over the new mutant allele. Furthermore, as individuals are better able to accommodate the presence and suppress the action of recessive genes when they are in a heterozygous situation, such genes are more likely to be carried in a greater proportion of the population. However, their often deleterious effect when they are in the homozygous state is sufficient to ensure that in the natural environment selective pressures will then proceed to act against homozygotes. It follows that a large number of the aberrations to be found in nature, and thus appear in this book, are due to genes essentially of a recessive nature.

The magnificent black ab. *obscura* Frohawk in the Swallowtail (Plate 4) is known to be controlled by a single recessive gene and it follows a specimen of this aberration must carry identical alleles coding for the character - a double dose as it were. In genetics it is conventional to use the first letter of the character (or aberrational name if one exists) to denote the particular feature being studied. In this instance, the capital letters *OO* can be used to represent the dominant alleles of the typical form and the same letters, but in lower-case i.e. *oo* for the recessive alleles that determine or code for *obscura*. The alleles carried by the progeny of the F_1 generation will be heterozygous and are represented as *Oo* (Diagram 1). A Swallowtail which is heterozygous for *obscura* is identical in appearance to the typical form in which the alleles controlling the normal ground colour are homozygous. Diagram 2 is a representation of this monohybrid cross.

By using Mendel's methods, confirmation that *obscura* is determined by a recessive gene can be established by breeding it through to the F_2 generation when it should reappear in approximately a quarter of the progeny. These aberrations will be homozygous for the *obscura* gene and paired together will result in a pure strain of the aberration in the F_3 generation.

Occasionally, when breeding from an aberration, it may appear in the F_1 generation. Should this occur, it need not necessarily imply that the gene for the character is dominant. The original female may have mated with a male heterozygous for the same gene and in discussing the Ringlet in the next chapter, I mention just such an instance happening. The ratios arising from further inbreeding will confirm the true situation.

In *Aberrations of British Butterflies* (Plate 5, fig. 1) an aberration in the Wood White, ab. *brunneomaculata* Stauder, is featured. The normal greyish black shading to the wings is replaced by a pale sandy brown or ochreous-buff. This has been bred and shown to be a simple recessive (Payne, 1981). In the Green-veined White, *Pieris napi britannica* Müller & Kautz, ab. *fasciata* Kautz and the beautiful yellow form ab. *sulphurea* Schöyen, illustrated here on Plate 7, figs 2, 5 and 6, have also proved to be simple recessives (Ford, 1945). The Brown Argus, *Aricia agestis* ([Denis & Schiffermüller]) sometimes has the upperside marginal lunules yellow instead of orange or red: ab. *pallidior* Oberthür (Plate 18, fig. 1). This likewise is controlled by a recessive gene (Jones, 1996). Similar in appearance to ab. *cinnameus* Bright & Leeds on Plate 21, figs 3, 4 in this book, the colour forms ab. *livida* Bright & Leeds in the male Chalk Hill Blue and its female equivalent, ab. *khaki* Bright & Leeds, have been found to be recessive in character, through breeding (Jones, 1992). The Gatekeeper, *Pyronia tithonus britanniae* Verity produces the beautiful colour form ab. *mincki* Seebold, in which the red-brown ground colour is replaced by yellow, closely resembling ab. *subalbida* Verity on Plate 77, figs 1, 2; it is recessive in character (Revels, pers. comm.). On rare occasions, the normal coloration in the Ringlet is replaced by yellow-brown (ab. *pallens* Schultz) and this aberration has similarly been shown to be due to a recessive gene (Revels, 1975b). Further examples of aberrations due to recessive genes are given in the next chapter.

MONOHYBRID INHERITANCE:
DOMINANT GENES (SINGLE GENE DIFFERENCE)

Where a single gene is responsible for a particular aberration being dominant, that aberration should appear in approximately half of the F_1 generation. These aberrant forms will be heterozygous and sibling pairings usually result in a ratio somewhere in the order of three aberration to, one typical form in the F_2 generation.

It would be logical to expect that a dominant gene arising by mutation would spread rapidly through a population to become the prevalent form. This is far from being the case - at least as far as butterflies are concerned. It is not obvious what practical advantages such dominant mutant genes could confer on the adult insect and indeed the situation is quite possibly the reverse. Ford suspected that in the homozygous dominant state, the adults were probably sub-viable. While these statements may be true for butterflies, it should be recognized that in some moths the majority of industrial melanics are controlled by single dominant genes. The increase and spread in the past 150 years of the black form f. *carbonaria* Jordan in the Peppered Moth, *Biston betularia* (L.), is a case in point. Several comprehensive treatments of the subject of melanism in insects, particularly in moths, are listed in the bibliography.

Returning to butterflies and the failure of dominant mutation to become the prevalent form, this phenomenon can be observed in the well-known polymorphic females of the Clouded Yellow form *helice* Hübner and the Silver-washed Fritillary form *valesina* Esper. When referring to polymorphism 'the existence together in the same habitat of two or more forms of a species none of which is relatively very rare' (Ford, 1945), the word 'form' or the abbreviation 'f.' is used instead of aberration to describe the polymorphic individual. Both these forms arise from dominant autosomal genes carried by both sexes and their mode of transmission is along Mendelian lines. However, the visual effect is only observed in the female; the gene is unable to express itself in the males even when in the homozygous state. This type of inheritance in which a gene can only find expression in one of the sexes is termed *sex-limited* or *sex-controlled inheritance* and is discussed further on. From breeding experiments neither of these two dominant genes appear to have any obvious harmful or weakening effect and yet both *helice* and *valesina* always remain as a low percentage of the overall population. In *Ecological Genetics*, Ford (1975) mentions 'it is generally agreed by entomologists that the habits of the two female forms of the Silver-washed Fritillary are distinguishable. The normal one is to be found particularly in sunny clearings and pathways while *valesina* is more restricted to the shade of overhanging trees.' It is probable that the genes coding for form *valesina* may affect not only wing colour but also flight pattern and possibly courtship. Similarly, in *Colias eurytheme* Boisduval, studied in North America, the '*helice*' or white forms were found to be active earlier in the morning than the typical form with the activity of both colour forms increasing towards noon, but the white ones being less affected, their activity tending to rise in the evening. This behaviour lengthens the period but reduces the degree of the insect's activity (Hovanitz, 1948).

♀ ab. *lugens* × ♂ typical

Parents (P₁)   L *l*   *l l*

Gametes

F₁ generation: 50% are ab. *lugens*

L *l* × L *l*   *l l* × *l l*

ab. *lugens*   ab. *lugens*   typical   typical

Gametes

male gametes

F₂ generation

	L	*l*
L	L L ab. *lugens* (homozygote)	L *l* ab. *lugens* (heterozygote)
l	L *l* ab. *lugens* (heterozygote)	*l l* typical

female gametes

F₂ generation should produce ratio of 3 ab. *lugens* (including 1 homozygote) : 1 typical

DIAGRAM 3
MONOHYBRID INHERITANCE: SINGLE DOMINANT GENE DIFFERENCE

Mode of transmission of the dominant allele for ab. *lugens* Oberthür in the Gatekeeper, *Pyronia tithonus britanniae* (Verity)

This mechanism of inheritance can be applied to several other aberrations determined by dominant genes. In the Marbled White, *Melanargia galathea serena* Verity, the heterozygous ab. *aperta* Rebel can be distinguished from the slightly more extreme homozygous ab. *mosleyi* Oberthür. The resulting ratio in the F₂ generation would be 1 (*mosleyi*) : 2 (*aperta*) : 1 (typical).

Both f. *valesina* Esper, in the Silver-washed Fritillary, *Argynnis paphia* (L.) and f. *helice* Hübner in the Clouded Yellow, *Colias croceus* Fourcroy are controlled by dominant genes. However, in both cases the observable expression of the gene is seen in the female sex only i.e. it is sex-limited or sex-controlled, the effect being that in the F₁ generation the normal 1 : 1 (aberration to typical) ratio for dominant gene inheritance is modified to 2 (typical males) : 1 (typical female) : 1 (*helice/valesina* female). As there are no observable differences between heterozygotes and homozygotes in either sex and no lethality associated with the homozygous state, the F₂ generation will give a modified ratio in the order of 4 (typical males): 1 (typical female): 3 (*helice/valesina* females).

An alternative method of representing the F₂ generation has been used: the Punnet square. It was devised by the Cambridge geneticist Reginald Punnett.

Breeding experiments carried out by Nigel Potter and Les Young (1965) have established that ab. *disco-juncta* Tutt in the Small Copper, in which the two discal spots on the underside of the forewing are joined by a longitudinal line, was due to a dominant gene. An aberration very similar to this but slightly more extreme, ab. *anticentrijuncta* Leeds, is illustrated on Plate 14 (fig. 6). There is evidence to suggest that in the Common Blue the following underside forms are inherited on a dominant basis: *arcuata* Weymer, *costajuncta* Tutt, and *basijuncta* Tutt (Robertson & Young, 1984); also *transiens* Tutt and *elongata* Tutt (the last two corresponding in appearance to ab. *antidiscoelongata* B & L and ab. *basielongata* B & L respectively, in the Chalk Hill Blue) (Barrington and Young, 1990).

An extremely rare aberration in the Gatekeeper has the black borders to the forewings much widened, reaching beyond the apical spot. The hindwings are almost completely black-brown. Richard Revels (1998a) has successfully bred ab. *lugens* Oberthür (Charles) (page 90, a) through several generations and shown it to be controlled by a dominant gene. The outcome of a pairing between this aberration (represented by the letter L) and the typical form is set out in Diagram 3.

The diagram shows that three quarters of the F_2 generation produced are aberrant with a 2 : 1 ratio of heterozygote to homozygotes. In the case of ab. *lugens* these two genotypes are indistinguishable. This type of situation is referred to as *complete* (or *simple*) *dominance*. However, there are occasions when the homozygote is recognizably more extreme than the heterozygote. The term *incomplete dominance* (*semi-dominance*, or *partial dominance*) is used in instances where the heterozygote exhibits a phenotype intermediate between the two homozygous forms (*ll* and *LL*). Usually, the heterozygote is closer in appearance to the aberrant homozygote than the typical form.

Several of the most striking aberrations encountered in the Marbled White are determined by semi-dominant genes. In some instances the two forms have been separately named: ab. *mosleyi* Oberthür (Plate 71) is the homozygote of the heterozygote ab. *aperta* Rebel (Collier, 1955). The impressive heterozygote of ab. *nigricans* Culot (figured on Plate 72, figs 1, 2) is surpassed by its magnificent homozygous form, in which the discal cell to the forewing is almost totally suffused with black scaling, accompanied by an extension of the areas of black on the hindwings (Barrington, 1999c).

In ab. *craskei* Tubbs the central costal blotch extends outwards along the costa to join the sub-apical bar, and distally to become confluent with the marginal markings. It has a homozygote form. The aberration was first discovered by Robert Craske in two restricted localities in Sussex and Hampshire, in the 1970s (Tubbs, 1978b).

In the Cinnabar moth (page 47), ab. *coneyi* Watson also happens to be controlled by a dominant gene (Watson, 1967b).

DIHYBRID INHERITANCE
(DOUBLE RECESSIVE GENE DIFFERENCES)

THE same principles established in monohybrid inheritance apply equally when two differing characters are brought together in a dihybrid cross. Aberrations are uncommon enough at the best of times; to find a butterfly that displays two separate aberrant characters is extremely rare. Amongst our native species, the Small Copper is arguably unequalled in terms of recessive aberrant genes that lend themselves to this particular form of study. In *Butterflies*, Ford had to use a hypothetical instance to represent his example of a dihybrid cross, selecting ab. *alba* Tutt (= ab. *schmidtii* Gerhardt) and ab. *obsoleta* Tutt in the Small Copper, illustrated here on Plate 13, figs 1, 2; and Plate 14, fig. 2. I am indebted to Tom S. Robertson for being able to cite an actual example and one very similar to Ford's. In 1991 he carried out a dihybrid cross involving the two recessives ab. *radiata* Tutt (Plate 14, fig. 1) and ab. *pallidula* Leeds (= ab. *intermedia* Tutt) (Robertson, 1995a); the latter being similar to ab. *cuprinus* Peyerimhoff (Plate 13, figs 3, 4) but a less brilliant brassy yellow. Diagrams 4 and 5 explain how the alleles are transmitted. The recessive alleles for *radiata* are represented by *rr* and those for *pallidula* by *pp*. The results confirm Mendel's Law of Independent Segregation, demonstrating that the alleles of the two genes are transmitted independently of each other from parents to offspring, and may combine independently with each of the alleles of another gene.

DIAGRAM 4

MEIOSIS AND MENDEL'S LAW OF INDEPENDENT ASSORTMENT

Independent assortment in a pairing between ab. *pallidula* Leeds and ab. *radiata* Tutt in the Small Copper, *Lycaena phlaeas eleus* (Fabricius)

The diagram opposite represents certain stages in meiosis that explain how, during gamete production in the F_1 progeny (Diagram 5), the random and independent orientatation of the bivalents about the equator of the spindle results in the production of four kinds of gametes by each parent. Independent assortment can only occur if the alleles of *pallidula* and *radiata* are carried on different chromosomes. In a pairing between F_1 progeny the gametes randomly combine with each other. Consequently, in addition to the original parental forms reappearing in the F_2 generation, two new combinations - typical and ab. *pallidula* Leeds + *radiata* Tutt - are also produced.

(**i**) Chromosomes in the cells in the reproductive organs contract, thicken and become visible, (**ii**) the homologous chromosomes pair up to form bivalents, (**iii**) each chromosome has replicated longitudinally and is seen to consist of a pair of sister chromatids, (**iv**) two alternative arrangements of the chromatids are possible as bivalents randomly orientate themselves around the equator of the spindle which has formed, attaching themselves to the spindle fibres; the wall of the nucleus breaks down, (**v**) first cellular division in meiosis begins and chromatids start to pull apart from each other and migrate to opposite poles of the cell and cleavage of the cell begins, (**vi**) two intermediate cells are formed and the nuclear wall reforms, (**vii**) the second division (essentially mitotic in nature) in meiosis commences, the nuclear wall breaks down and chromatids arrange themselves on the spindle again, pull apart from each other and migrate to opposite poles of the cell, again accompanied by cell cleavage, (**viii**) four daughter cells created which are the gametes (eggs or sperms). Four different kinds of gamete are produced, in approximately equal frequencies. Each gamete only contains a single set of chromosomes i.e. they are haploid. The full or diploid number of chromosomes is restored by the fusion or fertilization of two gametes to form a zygote.

For the purposes of simplification, only the chromatids for the two recessive genes are shown; the other chromosome pairs are omitted. The crossing over that sometimes occurs between homologous chromosomes, and the cell cytoplasm, have also been omitted.

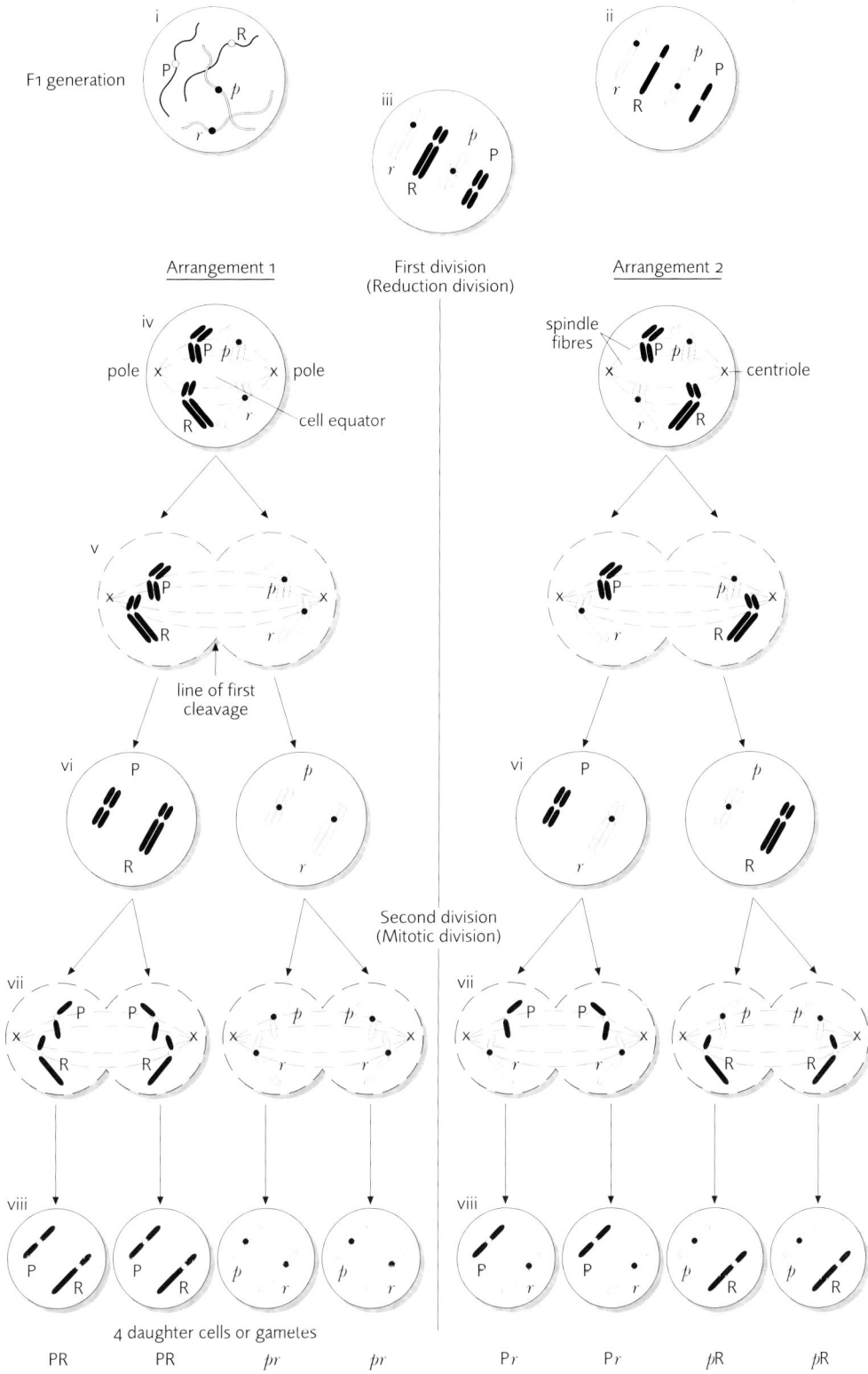

F1 generation

i

ii

iii

Arrangement 1

First division
(Reduction division)

Arrangement 2

iv

pole x   x pole

cell equator

spindle
fibres

x   x centriole

v

line of first
cleavage

vi   P   p   vi   P   p

R   r   R   r

Second division
(Mitotic division)

vii   vii

viii   viii

4 daughter cells or gametes

PR   PR   pr   pr   Pr   Pr   pR   pR

Note: Both male and female produce 4 different gametes each of which can randomly pair with each other.

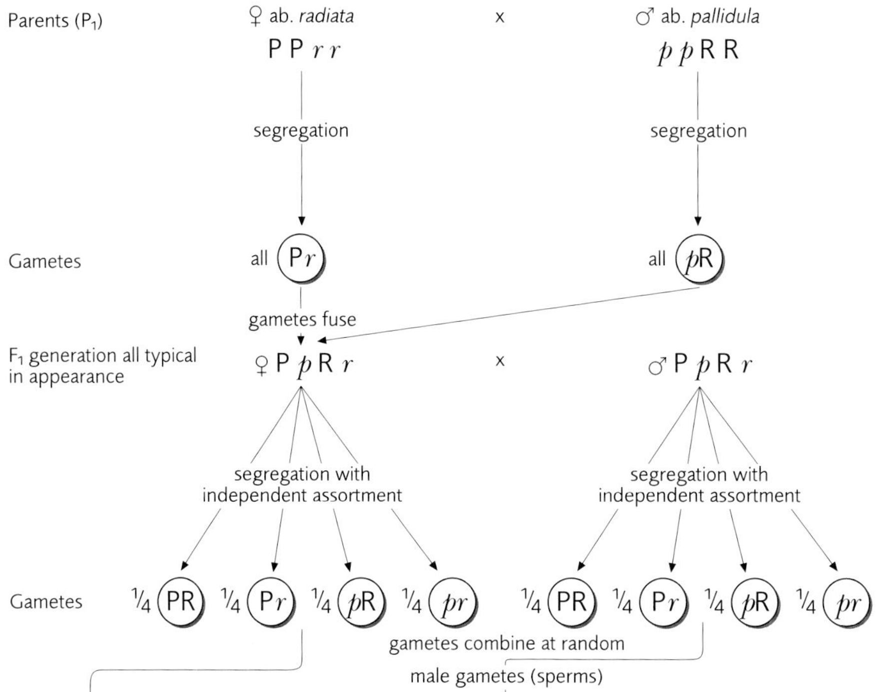

Parents (P_1)
♀ ab. *radiata*
P P *r r*
x
♂ ab. *pallidula*
p p R R
segregation
segregation
Gametes
all P*r*
all *p*R
gametes fuse
F_1 generation all typical in appearance
♀ P *p* R *r*
x
♂ P *p* R *r*
segregation with independent assortment
segregation with independent assortment
Gametes
¼ PR ¼ P*r* ¼ *p*R ¼ *pr*
¼ PR ¼ P*r* ¼ *p*R ¼ *pr*
gametes combine at random
male gametes (sperms)
female gametes (egg cells)
F_2 generation

	¼ PR	¼ P*r*	¼ *p*R	¼ *pr*
¼ PR	P P R R 1⁄16 typical	P P R *r* 1⁄16 typical	P *p* R R 1⁄16 typical	P *p* R *r* 1⁄16 typical
¼ P*r*	P P R *r* 1⁄16 typical	P P *r r* 1⁄16 ab. *radiata*	P *p* R *r* 1⁄16 typical	P *p r r* 1⁄16 ab. *radiata*
¼ *p*R	P *p* R R 1⁄16 typical	P *p* R *r* 1⁄16 typical	*p p* R R 1⁄16 ab. *pallidula*	*p p* R *r* 1⁄16 ab. *pallidula*
¼ *pr*	P *p* R *r* 1⁄16 typical	P *p r r* 1⁄16 ab. *radiata*	*p p* R *r* 1⁄16 ab. *pallidula*	*p p r r* 1⁄16 ab. *pallidula* + ab. *radiata*

F_2 phenotypes 9⁄16 typical: 3⁄16 ab. *pallidula*: 3⁄16 ab. *radiata*: 1⁄16 ab. *pallidula* + *radiata*

DIAGRAM 5

DIHYBRID INHERITANCE: DOUBLE RECESSIVE GENE DIFFERENCES

Mode of transmission of two pairs of recessive alleles each controlling a pair of contrasting characters in the Small Copper, *Lycaena phlaeas eleus* (Fabricius)

Both ab. *pallidula* Leeds and ab. *radiata* Tutt are determined by recessive genes. For the purposes of clarity, a Punnett square has been used to depict the results in the F_2 generation, avoiding the use of numerous criss-crossing lines. The results confirm Mendel's Law of Independent Assortment i.e. two or more pairs of contrasted characters involved in the same cross may segregate independently of each other and may combine randomly with either of another pair, provided the characters concerned are not located on the same chromosome i.e. they are unlinked.

DISCONTINUOUS VARIATION

ALL the different mechanisms of inheritance described so far have involved characters determined on a unifactorial basis by the alleles of a single recessive or dominant gene, conforming to Mendel's laws. The characters expressed are quite distinctive in appearance from the normal or typical form and display what is termed *qualitative variation* i.e. the aberrant forms are clearly recognizable by the particular qualities they express, e.g. wing ground colour. Because the individual genes concerned have such an obvious and clear-cut effect upon the phenotype, they are sometimes referred to as *major genes*. This type of variation, in which the two alternative expressions of a given character are readily identifiable and easily grouped with no intermediate forms being produced, is described as *discontinuous variation*. However, lepidopterists will have observed that even in aberrations where the expression of a character is determined by a single pair of alleles, a discernible amount of minor variation is invariably present. This minor variation can be ascribed to the presence of other genes, each varying or modifying the exact expression of the major gene to a small degree in either direction. They are known as *modifying genes*. By selectively breeding from the more extreme aberrant specimens each time, the effects of these modifying genes can be reduced, making further intensification of the desired feature possible. Notwithstanding this minor degree of variable expression between individuals, the characters always remain clearly distinguishable.

CONTINUOUS VARIATION

UNLIKE the characters studied by Mendel, very often a particular feature is not determined solely by a single gene. Within a series of butterflies bred for a particular aberration, it is often apparent that the desired character is not expressed to anything like the same extent in every insect. Although there may be considerable variation over the entire range, the intermediate individuals between the two extremes display only marginal differences in relation to each other, giving the effect of merging into one another to produce a continuum. There are no separate or discrete forms; individuals can only be graded on a quantitative basis e.g. by measurement of spot size. This slight gradation in which there are no clearly defined separate forms is known as *continuous or quantitative variation*. Human height is a good example of this type of variation.

Continuous variation occurs when two or more genes act together to determine a single character e.g. wing spot size. The contribution made by each of these genes is small and approximately equal but their interaction with one another has a cumulative or additive effect - often quite markedly so. The extent of this expression will depend on the number of dominant or recessive alleles present in the genes involved. For example, let us assume that the character for wing spot size is determined by two genes, each on a different chromosome and each having two alleles. The genotype of the parents could extend from *aabb* (normal spotting) through to *AABB* (extreme wing spot development). A pairing between two such homozygous individuals would produce a heterozygous F_1, their genotype being *AaBb*. Each dominant allele present can be considered as contributing a positive or additive effect to wing spot size and given an arbitrary value of one unit and each recessive allele present in the individual a value of zero. Accordingly, *AABB* would have a maximum value of four units, *aabb* a value of zero, *AaBb* a value of two units and so on. To give some idea of the extent of variation possible the independent segregation of just two pairs of alleles from a sibling pairing of the F_1 individuals will give rise to nine possible genotypes in the F_2. These divide into five phenotypic classes or grades with their values ranging from zero through to four. One in sixteen of the progeny would be homozygous for all alleles (either *AABB* or *aabb*) and therefore identical to one or other of the parents. The other fourteen out of sixteen would be intermediates.

Should an additional gene be involved in determining the same character, then seven phenotypic classes would be distinguishable in the F_2. This time only one in sixty-four of the progeny would be genetically identical to either parent. The remaining sixty-two out of sixty-four would be intermediates. By selectively breeding each time from the most extreme examples containing the highest proportion of allelomorphs in the homozygous state, the varietal characters can be intensified still further. Eventually, it is possible to obtain an almost pure-breeding line of these extreme forms. In many of the breeding experiments I have mentioned, commendable foresight was shown by the individuals concerned in recognizing the potential in the aberrations they initially selected for breeding. They were prepared to devote time and effort on the off chance that their optimism might be rewarded. They demonstrated that, by starting with the most unpromising of aberrations and using this selection technique, dramatic results can be achieved within a couple of generations.

MULTIFACTORIAL INHERITANCE

Genes associated with continuous variation are transmitted in Mendelian fashion. The results, however, will not produce Mendelian ratios. In continuous variation, several genes control a single character, whereas in Mendelism, several characters are each controlled by a single gene. The transmission of characters controlled by more than one gene is known as *multifactorial* or *polygenic inheritance*. For the breeder the study and analysis of quantitative inheritance is complicated by the fact that it is usually very difficult to identify either the numbers or the individual genes involved. Furthermore, their individual contributions, having only a small effect, may be obscured by interaction with internal and external environmental influences.

Much of the variation encountered in our butterflies, perhaps most noticeably demonstrated in the Lycaenidae and Satyridae, emanates from this form of inheritance in which several genes are involved in the determination of an observable character. The two particular families mentioned offer enormous genetic opportunities to the collector.

It would be naïve to expect that continuous and discontinuous variation are at all times clearly separable from each other. Indeed, it would be more than reasonable to assume that, given the enormous numbers of genes present plus the individual and collective interactions between them, ample scope exists for gradation between these two modes of inheritance. The Grayling population on Portland provides an intriguing and convenient case in point, illustrating as it does the problems that face the breeder investigating these two phenomena.

I have found in specimens from this locality that the forewing spotting is given to a considerable range of variation both in respect to size and number of ocelli, and to the degree of development of pupillation. Individuals include those with enlarged spotting (ab. *macrocellata* Lempke); an additional forewing spot either above or below the normal lower ocellus (ab. *tripuncta* Tutt); reduction in spot size to little black points (ab. *thyone* Schultz, Plate 75, fig. 2); reduction in spot number (ab. *monocellata* Lempke, Plate 73, fig. 3 and Plate 74, fig. 3); and finally, complete absence of ocelli from all wings, both upper and underside (ab. *holonops* Brouwer, Plate 75, fig. 1). There may indeed be other aberrations. As far as I am aware, only limited genetic investigation has been undertaken into these different forms. I would suggest that here several (as opposed to one) disparate groups of genes are operating on a multifactorial inheritance basis, but that the last three named aberrations are linked, controlled by a recessive gene acted upon by modifying genes. I am indebted to Richard Revels for what insight we do have into this genetic conundrum. Breeding from a captured female closely approaching *holonops*, except for a minute black apical spot on the upper and underside of the forewing, he has established that *holonops* is recessive in character, with the F₁ generation being typical. The aberration appeared below the expected Mendelian ratio of 3 : 1 in the subsequent F₂ generation, producing 31 typical; 2 *holonops* (females); 1 *monocellata* (female); plus an unnamed aberrant male which had the apical spot missing and was thought not to be connected to the *holonops* gene. The results suggested that the gene had a debilitating effect (Revels, 1978; Tubbs, 1978a). In a subsequent attempt at breeding from a female *monocellata* by Richard Revels, he obtained ten typical specimens in the F₁ generation. Three of these females were used to out-cross with three wild male *monocellata*. Six hundred ova were laid and the hundred progeny in the F₁ generation produced the following results: 34 *monocellata* males; 18 females with forewing spotting much reduced and only one forewing spot on the underside; 48 mostly typical but with some having three forewing spots. Colour forms also appeared but no *holonops* forms were obtained (pers. comm.). The 1 : 1 ratio of typical specimens to those either tending towards or which are *monocellata*, accords with what would be expected from a pairing between a heterozygote and a homozygote recessive.

In the Gatekeeper, the forewing apical spot is frequently accompanied by extra spotting. This aberrant form is referred to as ab. *excessa* Tutt (Plate 77, figs 1, 2). The results obtained by Richard Revels when he bred this aberration through to the F₂ generation indicated that it was subject to multifactorial inheritance (Revels, 1977a).

In the Meadow Brown the variation both in the number, size and positioning of the small hindwing spots, and the size, shape and bipupillation of the forewing 'eye-spot' has been the subject of much intensive study by ecological geneticists (E. B. Ford, W. H. Dowdeswell, P. M. Brakefield, A. J. van Noordwijk and others). These features have been found to be controlled by many genes each exerting a small additive effect, and also, partly by the environment during development. A useful summary of this research is given in *The Moths and Butterflies of Great Britain and Ireland*, (Emmet & Heath, 1989) and a full account can be found in *The Life of the Meadow Brown* (Dowdeswell, 1981).

Over recent years, Rupert Barrington has had outstanding successes both in the field and with breeding some of the rare aberrations that occur in the Meadow Brown. His published articles also contain some useful tips on breeding this somewhat difficult species (Barrington, 1984, 1992a). In respect to additional upperside forewing spotting in ab. *addenda* Mousley, the conclusions from his experiments accord with those for underside spotting: that *addenda* is also inherited on a multifactorial basis. Extra spotting involving the upper and underside of the hindwings occurred in a few of the best *addenda* specimens suggesting that all the extra spotted forms may be associated in a multifactorial complex (Barrington, 1994a). He has found that the splendid ab. *postmultifidus* Lipscomb (Plate 79, figs 2, 3) is due to a dominant gene affected by a series of modifying genes which determine its expression. This gene also appears to reduce the fitness of butterflies that carry it. Another very striking aberration in this species in which the median band on the underside of the hindwing is divided in the middle (cell 4) by a dark stripe, cutting it into two parts, is named ab. *fracta* Zweigelt. Rupert Barrington has produced some fine examples of this aberration in an F_2 generation originating from a female transitional to *fracta* (Barrington, 1999a). His results suggest that the gene is multifactorially controlled and that it is more strongly expressed in the female. Another feature that seems to be associated with *fracta* is reduction in the width of the hindwing median band.

An idea of what can be achieved in multifactorial inheritance by selective breeding is beautifully illustrated on Plate 62, figs 3-6 in ab. *bicolor* Wehrti of the Marsh Fritillary. This aberration was the result of a breeding programme carried out by Mr J. Shepherd in which he consistently selected and paired the darkest individuals over fourteen generations, eventually producing a series of completely black specimens (Ford, 1945).

In the male Chalk Hill Blue, the normal border to the forewings is occasionally distinctly broader and darker: ab. *marginata* Tutt (= *inframarginata* Bright & Leeds). In a pairing obtained by Richard Revels (1975a) between a wild *marginata* male and a normal female, the resulting males in the F_1 generation had fairly good black margins, but were only transitional to *marginata*. These progeny were inbred and the F_2 generation included males with borders ranging from around typical width, to one specimen more extreme than *marginata*, having the marginal band extending along the costa from the apex down to the discoidal point: ab. *seminigra* Preissecker.

A final example of the benefits that may be obtained by employing this technique is provided in the experiments carried out by Les Young with the Common Blue (Barrington and Young, 1990). From two relatively minor examples of ab. *transiens* Tutt and ab. *elongata* Tutt, he succeeded in breeding some spectacular aberrations, including the unexpected bonus of a bilateral gynandromorph thrown in for good measure!

ENVIRONMENTAL ABERRATIONS

A LITTLE further on when sex-controlled inheritance is discussed, mention will be made of the fact that the particular internal environment of the cell can prevent the expression of certain characters. Similarly, the external environment can also have a modifying effect on gene expression.

For over a century it has been known that many of the extreme melanic aberrations which occur naturally in the Nymphalidae can be artificially produced by subjecting the early pupal stages to extremes of temperature for varying periods (Standfuss, 1900-01). Some of the most striking specimens that appear in this book are the rare melanic aberrations found in this family. The pigment melanin is responsible for the black and brown coloration of butterflies and is produced during development by the oxidation of the amino acid tyrosin - a colourless substance - through the action of an enzyme, tyrosinase. The extent of melanin deposition can be influenced by temperature: increased melanism in the Pieridae is associated with the spring generation, and the cooler conditions of high latitude or altitude (thermal melanism). In other species e.g. the Holly Blue, *Celastrina argiolus britanna*

(Verity) (Plate 28) the extent of melanin development in the summer generation is influenced by day length and temperature.

Evidence in support of environmental influence being a factor is to be found in *Varieties of British Butterflies*, wherein Frohawk cites certain years in which there was a comparative abundance of melanic aberrations in the New Forest. These seasons were often preceded by severe winters, followed by spells of almost tropical heat; the intervening years produced very little. In an article in *The Entomologist's Record and Journal of Variation* entitled *The New Forest in the 'Nineties and After* S. G. Castle Russell (1952) gives a vivid and exciting account of the famous seasons of 1918 and 1919. In addition to his own wonderful captures, he mentions an exhibit at the Entomological Society of over fifty extreme aberrations taken in the Forest in 1918 by Sir Vauncey Harpur Crewe and his assistants. Again in the *'Record'*, the Rev. J. N. Marcon gives a fascinating account of the sudden large numbers of aberrations that occurred in certain areas of the New Forest in 1941 and 1942 (Marcon, 1980b). He was aware of at least sixty-five Silver-washed Fritillary and thirty-one White Admiral aberrations being taken in the two seasons. Some of these marvellous captures are figured in this work. In the same journal, Major-General C. G. Lipscomb (1978) described a similar instance happening in Wiltshire in 1976, when at least thirty-five major aberrations were taken.

The events that bring about these periods of exceptional abundance in terms of population numbers and aberrations are not fully understood. Marcon mentioned what he considered to be an important factor that operated in two of these events, namely that they occurred during the World Wars, which limited the usual trimming of rides and the cutting of brambles in the New Forest. One possible explanation to account for all these extraordinary seasons is that they were preceded by favourable climatic conditions, causing a rapid increase in population numbers and a relaxation in selection pressures. As a result many 'low fitness' aberrations which would normally have been selected out of the population survived. In 1976 a similar population increase was also seen in the moths, again with more abnormal forms than usual being recorded (Majerus, 1998).

Melanism in the Pearl and Small Pearl-bordered Fritillary is attributed by Robert Craske to the heavy ground frosts that may occur well into May; the lowest contours in the localities he worked were always productive (pers. comm.). Between 1935-1958, he and his brother Jack collected nearly one hundred and seventy (including many extreme) aberrations of these two species in Chiddingfold and Dunsfold in Surrey, and also Abbot's Wood in Sussex, before these localities succumbed to coniferization. On three or four occasions in Abbot's Wood they took as many as six or eight fine aberrations of the Small Pearl-bordered Fritillary in a day. Such a remarkable achievement will never be surpassed. All these splendid captures are now in the National Collection.

Mr F. V. L. Jarvis has demonstrated that on the underside, forewing spot elongation and hindwing spot obsolescence in the Brown Argus, and the Northern Brown Argus, *Aricia artaxerxes artaxerxes* (Fabricius) could be induced by subjecting mature larvae and pupae to a period of low temperature i.e. around 2°C (Jarvis, 1958).

The extent of blue scaling in females of the Adonis Blue varies considerably and it has generally been noted as being more prevalent in the spring brood. Some idea of this gradation is shown in the two females on Plate 26, figs 7, 8. The forms ab. *ceronus* Esper and ab. *semiceronus* Tutt are equal in the development of blue scaling; the distinction being that in the latter, the orange marginal lunules are only present on the hindwings. Neither of these aberrations is the gene equivalent of *tithonus* in the Chalk Hill Blue as gradation in blue scaling in the Adonis Blue can be demonstrated from the typical brown female right through to *ceronus*. It is likely that its presence or absence is the result of genes whose influence is determined by environmental conditions - most probably cold. In the warm spring of 1990 (the driest and sunniest for one hundred and fifty years, according to my diary notes), I recorded the fact that in a Dorset population of the Adonis Blue visited in late May that year, there was an absence of these blue female forms.

Over the last few decades, Karl Bailey has specialized in the area of temperature experiments with considerable success, concentrating mainly on the Nymphalidae. With the exception of the Dark Green Fritillary, he has been successful in obtaining major aberrations in all the native species within this particular family. The temperatures employed range from as low as minus 8°C to over 40°C. In addition to the temperature shock treatment of young pupae during the first forty-eight hours, he has also experimented with the effect of day length on final instar larvae immediately prior to pupation. He has found that as a result of such treatment, pupae are often more responsive to the effects of subsequent cold shock. Perhaps certain critical biological functions are destabilised by such action at this vital stage of development. His research has indicated that ab. *klemensiewiczi* Schille in the Red Admiral (page 89, e); ab. *testudo* Esper, in the Large Tortoiseshell (Plate 41); and ab. *semiiichnusoides* Pronin in the Small Tortoiseshell (Plates 39 and 40, figs 1, 2), can all be induced using high temperature shock at the early pupal stage. Conversely, ab. *obliterae* Robson & Gardner (Plate 31) and ab. *nigrina* Weymer (Plate 32) in the White Admiral; ab. *confluens* Spuler, ab. *ocellata* Frings (Plates 54-58), ab. *nigrizina* Frohawk (Plate 57, figs 3, 4), and ab. *nigricans* Cosmovici, in the Silver-washed Fritillary (Plate 58, figs 2, 3); and ab. *elymi* Rambur in the Painted Lady (page 89, e), can be produced using cold temperature treatment. None of these melanic forms, however, appear to be heritable. A pairing between *nigrizina* and *confluens* in the Silver-washed Fritillary followed by subsequent cold temperature treatment of the pupae, failed to have any effect on the butterflies that emerged. It is interesting to note that the temperatures necessary to bring about all these aberrations appear to be far in excess of what can be expected during a British summer, even, perhaps, at a microclimatic level. There must be other factors involved (page 94).

In the Satyridae the effects of temperature have been studied in the Meadow Brown by George Thomson (1973) to determine the role played by environmental influences in the various geographical races of this species. He concluded that a temperature of 30°C reduced the fulvous markings on the upperside of the forewings and hindwings, but only within certain genetically determined limits. There was also an indication that the size of the apical eyespot was increased and the medial line on the underside of the forewings darkened, but not greatly or consistently. He concluded that while the effects of temperature can be seen in wild populations, the factors producing the known phenotypes of the geographical races are genetic and not environmental.

In the Speckled Wood, *Pararge aegeria tircis* (Godart), ab. *cockaynei* Goodson is environmentally controlled. I have produced this striking form by holding back early larval development until after Christmas, and then increasing the daylight length to 16 hours. The larvae were kept in an unheated room throughout the experiment. In the wild, frost as a factor in the occurrence of this form has been suggested (Winokur, 1995). This aberration is figured in *South's British Butterflies*: Plate 33, fig. 5 and *Aberrations of British Butterflies*: Plate 32, figs 2, 2a.

SEX DETERMINATION

QUITE often some of the most remarkable and noticeable characters in species are to be found in the differences that exist between the sexes. Sex in Lepidoptera is an inherited character, passed on in similar Mendelian fashion to those considered earlier, producing ratios of males to females in approximately equal proportions. The next four categories have a commonality in so far as they are all intrinsically associated with either the determination or the inheritance of sex, each demonstrating a different aspect of the developmental process. Their mode of function will be better understood if the method by which sex is transmitted is first explained.

Previously, in discussing cells and cell structure, it was stated that the pairs of chromosome in a cell are homologous, with the exception of the sex chromosomes. The sex of an individual is determined by the sex chromosomes, which are found in

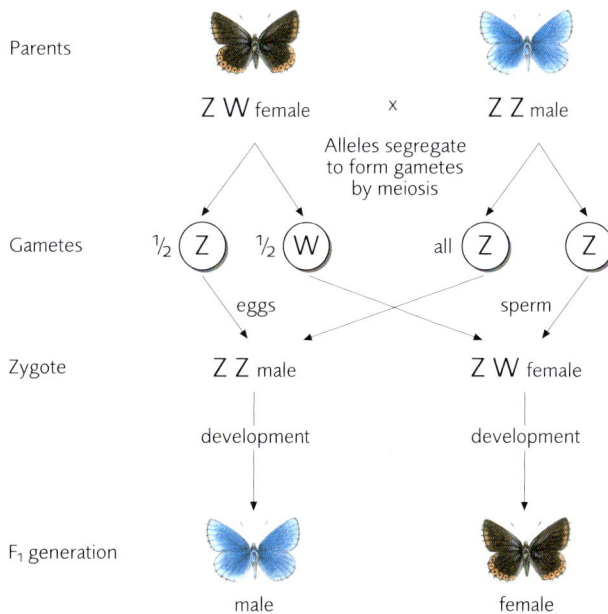

DIAGRAM 6

SEX INHERITANCE

The Adonis Blue, *Lysandra bellargus* (Rottemburg)

Like other characteristics, sex is also inherited and transmitted in Mendelian fashion and the ratio between the sexes is approximately equal. The genes responsible for determining sex are carried on the sex-chromosomes. In Lepidoptera, it is the number of Z chromosomes present in the zygote that determines the sex. The male has two Z chromosomes and is referred to as the homogametic sex. The female has one Z chromosome and one W chromosome. Although the W chromosome carries few genes and is generally not concerned with sex determination, its importance in Lepidoptera has yet to be fully determined. (The fractions indicate that half of the gametes will each contain either the Z or W chromosome.)

every cell of the insect's body. In each cell of a male butterfly both these chromosomes are alike and are termed the *Z chromosomes* and represented by ZZ, but in the female they differ: there is only one Z chromosome, the other one of this dissimilar pair is referred to as the *W chromosome*; it is shorter, carries very few genes and no sex-controlling genes. These female sex chromosomes are represented by the letters ZW. The presence or absence (due to loss through abnormal cell division) of the W chromosome appears to have no role in sex determination. However, it should be emphasized that its importance has not been fully determined in Lepidoptera and it may yet prove to carry some female-determining genes (Robinson, 1971).

The sex of a butterfly is determined by the number of Z chromosomes it inherits (Diagram 6). If there are two Z chromosomes present, the resulting insect will be male; if only one is present, it will be female. In humans and other mammals and most insects other than Lepidoptera, the reverse situation is found. Here, the female is the one which has two similar sex chromosomes (XX) and the male unlike chromosomes (XY). To distinguish between these different systems of sex-determination where it is the male that carries two similar chromosomes and which is referred to as the *homogametic sex*, it is customary to employ other letters to denote the sex chromosomes. In butterflies and moths (and birds), the X is represented by Z, and the Y is represented by W.

'The main function of the sex chromosomes is to act as a "switching device" and to direct the developmental process along one of the two alternative pathways' (Jones and Karp, 1986). As the Z chromosomes are constantly shuffled across from one sex to the other, they cannot carry genes for the respective sexes and so their action must be quantitative. Most of the genes involved in the sex-determining process are found in the autosomal chromosomes. In Lepidoptera sex determination is based on a balance in the ratio between the numbers of these autosomal sets and the number of Z chromosomes present in the cell. The effects that can arise should an imbalance in this ratio occur is discussed further on under Intersex.

SEX-LIMITED OR SEX-CONTROLLED INHERITANCE

ALTHOUGH this form of inheritance is only represented incidentally in this book (Plate 60, figs 1, 2), its inclusion here is important, nevertheless, by the manner in which this form of inheritance affects Mendelian ratios. The term 'sex-limited inheritance' refers to situations where the effects of a gene can find expression in only one of the sexes. Hence this phenomenon is also called *sex-limited expression*. The expression or suppression of the gene is controlled in some way by the different genetic environments existing in the cells between the sexes. Despite our relatively small number of native and migrant species, we are fortunate to have amongst them two very well-known instances of this special type of inheritance: f. *helice* in the Clouded Yellow and f. *valesina* in the Silver-washed Fritillary. Both these forms only find expression in the female sex.

The forms *helice* and *valesina* are both controlled by a single dominant gene carried on the autosomes by both sexes and passed on to their progeny equally by both parents. However, the gene is only able to express itself in the females. If a typical male not carrying an allele for *helice* is paired with a female *helice*, the resulting progeny should contain males which are normal in appearance, and typical and *helice* females in roughly equal proportions. In 1984, breeding from f. *helice*, I obtained 54 males, 28 typical females and 31 *helice* - approximately a 2 : 1 : 1 ratio. These results confirm that the male she had paired with was not carrying the gene for *helice* (had he been, the ratio would have been 4 : 1 : 3). In 1986, a brood of 212 imagines from a typical female Clouded Yellow produced 109 males, 48 typical females and 55 *helice* (Harmer, 1987). In this instance, the male parent was heterozygous for the *helice* gene and again the 2 : 1 : 1 ratio was obtained. That the expected ratios were achieved on both occasions is evidence that at least in the heterozygous state this dominant gene appears to have no obvious harmful or weakening effect. The mode of transmission for these two particular dominant genes is described in Diagram 3. In addition, the above results demonstrate quite nicely the appoximately equal proportions of males to females expected in sex inheritance (Diagram 6).

Parents (P$_1$)   ♀ ab. *tithonus*   x   ♂ typical

$Z^t W$ $Z Z$

Gametes Z^t W Z Z

F$_1$ generation
all typical in
appearance

$Z^t Z$ $Z^t Z$ $Z W$ $Z W$
  ♂   ♂   ♀   ♀

pairing obtained

Gametes Z^t Z Z W

F$_2$ generation $Z^t Z$ $Z^t W$ $Z Z$ $Z W$
                ♂   ♀ ab.   ♂   ♀
             typical   *tithonus*   typical   typical

DIAGRAM 7

SEX-LINKED INHERITANCE

The Chalk Hill Blue, *Lysandra coridon* (Poda): ab. *tithonus* Meigen

The gene for ab. *tithonus* Meigen in the Chalk Hill Blue is inherited as a sex-linked and sex-limited recessive carried on the Z chromosome (represented by Z^t). All the males in the F$_1$ generation carry the *tithonus* gene but it is absent in the females. A sibling pairing produces an F$_2$ generation in which all the males are typical and half of the females are ab. *tithonus*. The Mendelian ratio of 3 (typical) : 1 (ab. *tithonus*) is present but distributed relative to sex.

Any male from the F$_1$ generation could be paired with an unrelated typical female and the progeny would contain ab. *tithonus* in 50% of the females. Such outcrossings, where the desired aberration is recoverable in the subsequent F$_1$ generation, are rare. Normally, outcrossing, often necessary for maintaining the viability of the breeding stock, results in the programme being set back by a generation.

SEX-LINKED INHERITANCE

AT THE TIME of writing *Butterflies*, E. B. Ford was unaware of an example of a sex-linked gene in British butterflies. Through the breeding experiments of Major A. E. Collier (1956b, 1958, 1959b), Ralph Tubbs (1978a) and also Richard Revels (1975a, 1998a), it has been established that both ab. *tithonus* Meigen (=*syngrapha* Keferstein) (page 88, e and Plate 23, figs 7, 8) and ab. *semisyngrapha* Tutt in the Chalk Hill Blue (Plate 23, figs 4-6), are examples of that very rare phenomenon, recessive genes which are both sex-linked and sex-limited. A different gene is responsible for each of these two distinct forms.

Whereas in sex-controlled inheritance the genes for *helice* and *valesina* are carried in the autosomes, in sex-linked inheritance the genes for the character are located in the sex chromosomes. In *tithonus* and *semisyngrapha* the genes responsible are carried on the Z chromosome in the aberrant female and are subsequently transmitted to the male offspring only. Only one allele of the aberrant gene can ever be present in the female due to the fact that the W chromosome does not contain the equivalent chromosomal portion found in the Z chromosome to allow the gene to locate itself on the W chromosome. Sibling pairings result in half the females in the F_2 generation being the aberrant form and half the males carrying the gene. Further confirmation of sex linkage is demonstrated when F_1 generation males are paired with unrelated, typical females. Half the resulting females are *tithonus*. Males which are homozygous for the *tithonus* gene are indistinguishable from typical and heterozygote males. The homozygote state seems to have no deleterious effect upon the male as approximately equal numbers of both sexes appear in the progeny resulting from a pairing between a male heterozygous for *tithonus* and a female *tithonus* (Collier, 1959b). Diagram 7 explains the genetic principle involved.

GYNANDROMORPHISM

THESE remaining categories of variation differ from those preceding inasmuch as they are the product of abnormalities which have occurred in development during mitotic (as opposed to meiotic) cell division. Thus they are not governed by the principles of heredity, although there is circumstantial evidence to indicate that some hereditary influences may be involved and breeding from these forms would certainly be worthwhile. Dr. Edward A. Cockayne made a particular study of these three categories, publishing many important papers during the first half of the last century (Cockayne, 1922, 1926 a and b, 1935, 1938). A brief description by him on the reasons for these three forms of variation can be found in *A Monograph of the British Aberrations of the Chalk-Hill Blue Butterfly* (Bright & Leeds, 1938).

In Man, the destiny of the reproductive glands to develop into either male (testes) or female (ovaries) is determined by the sex chromosomes. The sex of all other parts of the body is controlled indirectly by hormones produced by these glands. These hormones circulate through the body via the bloodstream. The sex chromosomes that are present in all the cells play no part in this process. In insects, however, the situation is very different.

In the early cellular developmental stages of butterflies the sex chromosomes present in every cell decide and control the sex of that particular part of the body. The sex of a butterfly is initially determined by the number of Z chromosomes present in the zygote: if two Z chromosomes are present it will be male; if only one it will be female. The zygote subsequently divides and each of these cells will go on

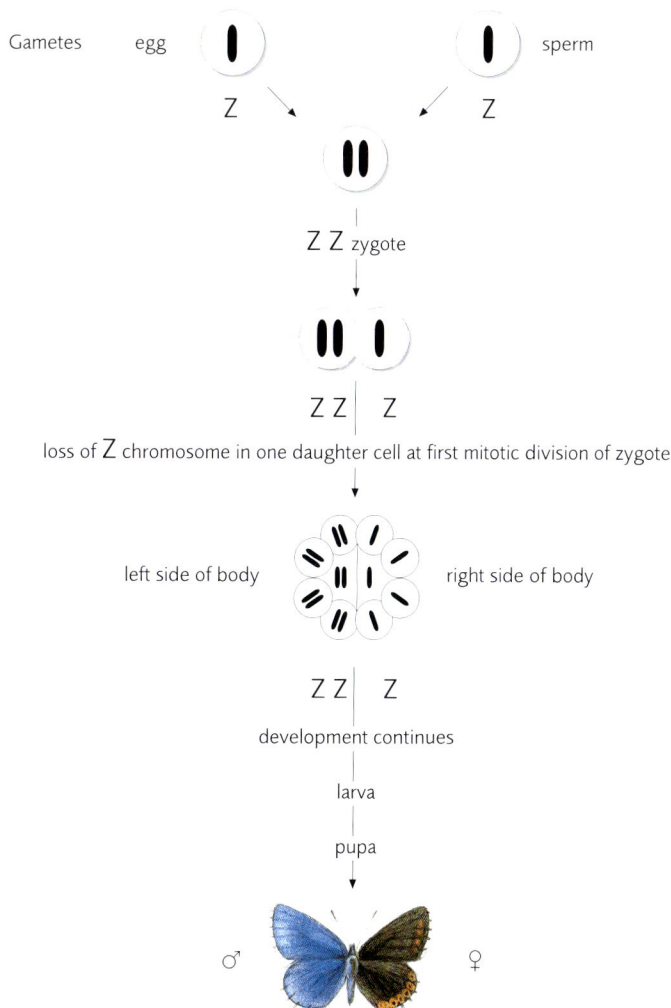

Gametes   egg   sperm

Z   Z

Z Z zygote

Z Z   Z

loss of Z chromosome in one daughter cell at first mitotic division of zygote

left side of body   right side of body

Z Z   Z

development continues

larva

pupa

♂   ♀

DIAGRAM 8

BILATERAL GYNANDROMORPHISM DUE TO CHROMOSOME LOSS AT FIRST CELL DIVISION

The Adonis Blue, *Lysandra bellargus* (Rottemburg)

In this instance, the zygote would have gone on to develop into a male Adonis Blue. However, the loss of the Z chromosome at the first mitotic division of the zygote results in the left side continuing to develop as a male, and the right side as a female.

For simplification, the autosomes (those chromosomes not involved with sex determination) have been omitted. (Adapted and redrawn from R. N. Jones and A. Karp: *Introducing Genetics.*)

to develop into the right and left sides of the body. At every cell division there is always a very small possibility of a Z chromosome being lost in the process, causing an imbalance between the autosomes and remaining sex chromosome. The resulting cell left with just one Z chromosome changes to being female in character and all further development is along those lines (Diagram 8). An individual which is composed of both male and female tissue is termed a *gynandromorph*. This is the most commonly accepted method by which gynandromorphs arise. Several alternative suggestions have been put forward to explain their origins including their developing from a binucleate ovum, each nucleus being fertilized by a different spermatozoon i.e. an egg that has two nuclei, one with ZZ chromosomes, the other ZW chromosomes (Cockayne, 1935, 1938). As some of these hypotheses are quite complex and have yet to be demonstrated in butterflies, they have not been included here. The phenomenon of gynandromorphism is represented in no less than ten species in this book: (page 89, a and b); Plates 6 (figs 1, 2); 8 (fig. 2); 19 (figs 1-4); 23 (figs 1, 2); 26 (figs 3-5); 28 (fig. 2); 30 (figs 3, 4); 59 (figs 1, 2); 60; and 70 (figs 5, 6).

Gynandromorphism is most often associated with wing coloration. Should these features appear combined on the same wing as a mosaic it is referred to as a *mixed gynandromorph*. But sometimes an insect is bisected, with one side of the body including the wings being either entirely male or entirely female. The exactness of the line of division is most effectively demonstrated when gynandromorphism occurs in some of the Blues. These remarkable and rare individuals are termed *bilateral gynandromorphs*. Certain butterflies such as the Orange-tip, *Anthocharis cardamines britannica* (Verity) and other subspecies, for example, the Common Blue, *Polyommatus icarus mariscolore* (Kane), appear more given to gynandromorphism, even accounting for the fact that it is obviously far more noticeable in these sexually dimorphic species. I referred to Don's capture of a bilateral gynandromorph Scotch Argus earlier on and a further example of good field observation is a bilateral gynandromorph White Admiral taken in Surrey in 1986 by George Beccaloni (Beccaloni, 1988). The Duke of Burgundy Fritillary, *Hamearis lucina* (L.) (Plate 30, figs 3, 4) emerged amongst stock being bred by John Turner.

INTERSEX

SUPERFICIALLY, intersexes can resemble gynandromorphs in their external appearance, particularly in those instances where the sexual mosaicism is not well-defined. They differ fundamentally from gynandromorphs in that, in the latter, after chromosome loss has occurred, the male and female cells develop in parallel. In intersex, development starts as being one particular sex but later on changes over to the opposite sex and continues development. This phenomenon is often associated with a disturbance to the normal balance between male and female-determining genes during development, resulting in adults that are more or less intermediate in structure between the two sexes.

Intersex is often noted as occurring in the progeny resulting from pairings between individuals of different races and species (hybridization). In these instances, the underlying cause has been described in *Lepidoptera Genetics* by Roy Robinson (1971) as being: ' . . . a physiological conflict between the relative potency of different Z and W chromosomes, against the general background influence of sets of autosomes'. By way of explanation, it has already been mentioned that in insects the sex chromosomes function mainly as a 'switching' device, directing the developmental process along either of the two - male/female - paths. Although they are the prime determinants, sex is usually a result of *dosage compensation*. Applied to Lepidoptera, dosage compensation refers to the balance between the male genes on the Z chromosomes and the female genes on the autosomes. The critical feature then is the ratio between the number of Z chromosomes and the number of sets of autosomes: (2 : 2 in males; 1 : 2 in females). Between different populations and species, these chromosomes may vary in their degree of effect upon the determination of maleness and femaleness. These differences will only become apparent when these races and species are crossed and the balance that formerly prevailed is upset.

There is evidence to suggest that intersex has some hereditary basis, recurring as it does in the same localities. For example, Royston Heath, in Hertfordshire, was well known for a particular form of intersex in the Chalk Hill Blue in which the female showed male scaling on one or more wings in a peppered manner, but never reaching the full scaling of the male. The wings affected were usually smaller. It was named after that famous locality: ab. *roystonensis* Pickett. It has also been noted that the occurrence of intersex forms is sometimes associated with large imbalances in the ratio of the sexes. In his paper entitled *Intersexes in the Lycaenidae*, Cockayne (1926b) mentions the great excess of female Chalk Hill Blues at Royston, the ratio estimated as varying between ten to fifty females to every male. He also cites Mr Castle Russell taking thirty-one intersexes in the Silver-studded Blue over a three day period in a Surrey locality, and in addition to these intersexes, 340 typical females were recorded by him. Remarkably though, not more than ten males were seen throughout the whole of the time. Roy Robinson (1971) has mentioned the possibility that some of these Lycaenid intersexes could indeed be complex gynandromorphs, on the basis that the male and female elements appear to occur in patches (indicative of gynandromorphism) and that they are not associated with inter-species crossing.

It has also been reported that intersexes often result after exposure to extreme temperatures when hormone production can be affected, disrupting the normal balance. In the fine summer of 1963, which followed one of the most severe winters recorded with unusually prolonged freezing temperatures, nine intersex aberrations of the Silver-studded Blue were taken at Chobham Common, Surrey by Mr R. F. Bretherton (1963). Intersex in this species is illustrated on Plate 16, figs 1-3.

HOMOEOSIS

Homoeosis is the term used to describe the phenomenon where one part of a body is converted into another part. It has been defined as 'a variation, which consists in the assumption by one member of a meristic series of the form and characters proper to other members of the series' (Bateson, 1894, 1900). In insects, the antennae, eyes (possibly), mouthparts and walking limbs constitute one meristic series - the wings another. In extreme cases, homoeosis can involve the substitution of complete wings for example, a forewing replacing a hindwing. In butterflies homoeosis is usually restricted to instances where areas of wing pattern or scaling are reproduced elsewhere on another wing. This transposition may involve any combination of wings including both dorsal and ventral surfaces. Most commonly in butterflies it is the ventral surfaces which are affected, with the associated transfer of wing scaling being confined to the same surface.

A useful compilation of data on wing homoeosis largely featuring specimens in the National Collection of Lepidoptera and in the collection of Mr L. Christie has been published by Atuhiro Sibatani (1983), and a very comprehensive review of homoeosis in the Small Copper has been carried out by Tom Robertson (1969-70, 1977). Two different forms of homoeosis in this species are featured in this book: page 87, d shows transference involving the same surfaces, from fore to hindwing (F/H homoeosis) and Plate 14, fig. 7 shows upperside coloration from the dorsal surface on the ventral surface (D/V homoeosis). Its appearance corresponds to ab. *inaequalis* Leeds which H. A. Leeds (1941) described from a female Small Copper which had the upperside left forewing showing a broad red streak via the discoidal spot, from the base to the outer border, blacking the latter as in the Chalk Hill Blue ab. *inaequalis* Tutt.

In his paper, Tom Robertson mentions two possibilities that might account for homoeosis: chromosomal change in a dividing cell, subsequently passed on to all the resulting daughter cells (somatic mutation); and 'leakage' of some external chemical (i.e. external to the group of cells) into an area where it should not have been. Such chemicals are sometimes called 'organizers' and might be enzymes or co-enzymes operating in an enzyme system. This leakage may be direct from the forewing to the hindwing, or indirect, being carried on the circulatory system during development.

While transposition of wing pattern as a result of homoeosis takes place in the later developmental stages and its influence is relatively limited, should homoeosis happen much earlier, its effect can be most dramatic. The importance of homoeosis has come to the fore in the last two decades with the discovery of certain single *developmental genes* responsible for controlling some of the early, fundamental stages of development. Should these genes mutate to become homoeotic, they are capable of causing huge developmental changes, creating a cascade effect. In the fruit fly (*Drosophila* species) for example, the mutation of a single gene - the 'bithorax gene' - causes a pair of wings to develop instead of the normal halteres (the gyroscopic sense organs). These findings are of extreme significance in that they challenge the very basis on which our concept of evolution is founded: that it has been a process of gradual change. Much of the homoeotic material that is available for research has been collected by British lepidopterists.

Chapter Five

Butterfly Genetics: in the Field

THE preceding chapter described in some detail the different mechanisms of inheritance that the collector is likely to come across. Now, drawing on my own collecting and breeding experiences and those of fellow lepidopterists, I include a selection of aberrations which demonstrate these genetic principles. The accompanying illustrations feature several aberrations that are either new or have not been previously photographed in life.

The Lulworth Skipper, *Thymelicus acteon* (Rottemburg)(page 87, a, b)

SCOPE for variation in this species is limited with only eight aberrations having been included in Goodson and Read (page xii); so any new forms are a most welcome addition. Recently, in a Dorset colony, I have come across in both sexes, individuals exhibiting a distinctive dark viridescent gold ground colour instead of the normal golden orange and olive. The closest approximation to any of the named forms I could find was ab. *alba* Bolton, relating to a female captured at Swanage in August 1950 by Ewart Bolton. He described his specimen as having the upperside ground colour black, with the crescentic band of linear markings on the forewings pure white, with greyish-yellow fringes (Bolton, 1950). My specimens did not appear black and the forewing markings were pale lemon yellow as opposed to pure white. The body hairs, particularly to the head and thorax, were a viridescent bluish green. I had noticed as they become worn, that specimens of this apparent new form appear black and the forewing markings become paler. Unfortunately, being unable to locate Bolton's specimen, closer comparison was not possible. The only help to hand was a black and white photograph of the specimen in the 1950-51 *Proceedings and Transactions of The South London Entomological and Natural History Society.* Despite some slight damage to the fringes, the insect appeared to be quite fresh.

The situation remained unresolved until Richard Revels sent me a photograph of the drawer of Lulworth Skippers in the National Collection. Straightaway, my attention was caught by a female at the bottom of the drawer. On the data label underneath the specimen could be made out a reference to 'page 63 *Entomologist*'; no aberrational description accompanied the specimen but this was undoubtedly the 'type' specimen. Looking up this reference proved my instinct had been correct and that this was the specimen which I had been so keen to find and whose true identity had been overlooked. Subsequent comparison at the museum confirmed that my specimens were ab. *alba*, notwithstanding Bolton's description.

Nearly fifty years after the original female was taken, this distinctive aberration, including the previously unknown male, is featured here for the first time. A short series will be donated to the National Collection. In the meantime, I am certain that the gene for *alba* will, on breeding, prove to be a simple recessive.

The Clouded Yellow, *Colias croceus* (Geoffroy) (page 87, c)

I CONFESS to a weakness for breeding the Clouded Yellow whenever the opportunity arises, especially the form *helice* in which the range of variation in the ground colour extends from white ab. *alba* Lempke through the creamy white of the true ab. *helice* Hübner, to the yellowish-orange of ab. *aubuissoni* Caradja. Being both a variable and an easy species to manage makes it a rewarding choice for the breeder; a good selection of the different aberrant forms can usually be obtained quite easily. Unfortunately, being continuously brooded, the opportunity for extended genetic research is somewhat restricted by our climate. Although, having said this, what is probably the first authenticated report of the larvae of this butterfly successfully overwintering (1998-9) on the South Coast, in the Bournemouth area, has just been published (Skelton, 1999). In my experience, specimens emerging in the autumn in captivity tend to be smaller and darker, no doubt as a result of the effect of decreasing day length and temperature during the larval stage.

Very occasionally, breeding from any typical butterfly can result in something totally unexpected. In August 1994, my son Arran captured a typical female Clouded Yellow near Lymington which I set up to breed. Amongst the resulting offspring that emerged in October were three males and one female of what appeared to be a completely new aberration, characterized by a complete absence of yellow and pink pigmentation. The ground colour to the upperside in both sexes was creamy white and on the underside the hindwings and borders of the forewings a creamy grey, creating a pale blue effect. The only female to emerge was slightly crippled and an attempt to breed from her proved unsuccessful.

The exact number of this aberration in the brood is not known. In addition to the three mentioned, about ten more failed to emerge completely or else experienced difficulty extricating their wings from the pupa. It was particularly dispiriting to have to stand by helplessly and witness this happen after having watched these beautiful butterflies colour up, their creamy forewings revealed through the pupal casing, and all the time anticipating a wonderful series of this unique aberration. It is estimated that the brood consisted of 12 normal males, 7 normal females, 11 (approximately) male aberrations, and 2 female aberrations. Allowing for the small sample size and the obviously unrepeatable nature of the event, one can only speculate on the genetics involved. Perhaps the simplest explanation is that it was the result of a single dominant gene blocking the yellow and pink pigment pathways, and that the unknown male which mated with the captured female was aberrant for that gene. The gene involved might well have been semi-lethal in both sexes, but more so in the female. The males that did succeed in emerging seemed rather weak. This hitherto unknown aberration has now been named ab. *russwurmi* Harmer (Harmer, 1999).

The Small Copper, *Lycaena phlaeas* (L.) (page 87, d - f)

TWO aberrant forms usually associated with the hindwing copper marginal band are ab. *radiata* Tutt and ab. *obsoleta* Tutt. (Plate 14, figs, 1 and 2). In the former, the normal copper marginal band is cut up into wedge-shaped streaks or rays, with their points towards the base. In *obsoleta*, this marginal band is entirely absent.

In the very hot summer of 1989, an aberration referable to ab. *partimauroradiata* Leeds, in which the marginal band is reduced and partly broken up into streaks, was

a. Lulworth Skipper, *T. acteon* (Rottemburg) male ab. *alba* Bolton.

c. Clouded Yellow, *C. croceus* (Geoffroy) male ab. *russwurmi* Harmer.

d. Small Copper, *L. phlaeas* (Fabricius) female - homoeosis.

e. Small Copper, *L. phlaeas* (Fabricius) male ab. *fuscae* Robson.

b. Lulworth Skipper, *T. acteon* (Rottemburg).

Left: typical male and female upper and undersides.

Right: ab. *alba* Bolton - male and female upper and undersides.

f. Small Copper, *L. phlaeas* (Fabricius) male ab. *obsoleta* Tutt.

Photos: Natural Image/Alec S. Harmer.

a. Common Blue, *P. icarus* (Rottemburg)
female ab. *radiata* Courvoisier.

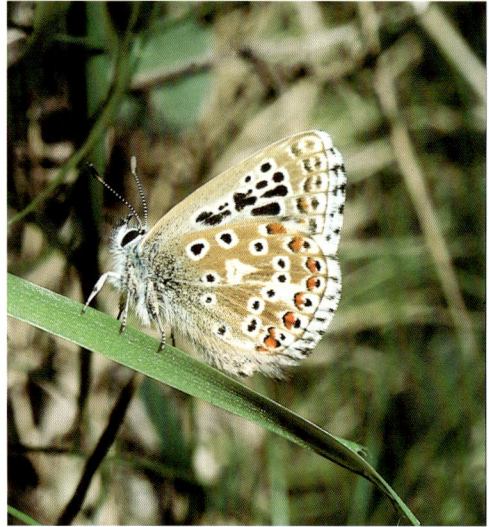

b. Adonis Blue, *L. bellargus* (Rottemburg)
male ab. *disco-juncta* Courvoisier.

c. Chalk Hill Blue, *L. coridon* (Poda)
female ab. *fowleri* South.

d. Chalk Hill Blue, *L. coridon* (Poda)
male ab. *ultrafowleri-margino* Bright & Leeds.

e. Chalk Hill Blue, *L. coridon* (Poda)
female ab. *tithonus* Meigen.

f. Chalk Hill Blue, *L. coridon* (Poda)
female ab. *tithonus* Meigen + *fowleri* South.

Photos: Natural Image/Alec S. Harmer.

a. Adonis Blue, *L. bellargus* (Rottemburg) mixed gynandromorph.

b. Meadow Brown, *M. jurtina insularis* Thomson bilateral gynandromorph.
Photo: Richard Revels and reproduced by kind permission.

c. Pearl-bordered Fritillary, *B. euphrosyne* (L.) female ab. *albinea* Lambillion.

d. Pearl-bordered Fritillary, *B. euphrosyne* (L.) female ab. *edna* Lobb.

e. Top: Red Admiral, *V. atalanta* (L.) female ab. *klemensiewiczi* Schille.

Bottom: Painted Lady, *C. cardui* (L.) female ab. *elymi* Rambur

Results of temperature shock treatment; a similar looking aberration in different species.

Photo: Karl Bailey and reproduced by kind permission.

f. Silver-washed Fritillary, *A. paphia* (L.) males. Result of temperature shock treatment. Aberrations that appear to be quite disparate may in fact be part of a continuous and progressive morphocline.

Photo: Karl Bailey and reproduced by kind permission.

Photos: Natural Image/Alec S. Harmer (unless otherwise stated).

a. Gatekeeper, *P. tithonus* (Verity)
female ab. *lugens* Oberthür (Charles).

Photo: Richard Revels and reproduced by kind
permission.

b. Meadow Brown, *M. jurtina insularis* Thomsoni
male ab. *anommata* Verity.

c. Ringlet, *A. hyperantus* (L.)
female ab. *arete* Müller.

d. Ringlet, *A. hyperantus* (L.)
female ab. *lanceolata* Shipp.

e. Ringlet, *A. hyperantus* (L.)
female ab. *lanceolata* Shipp + *arete* Müller.

f. Ringlet, *A. hyperantus* (L.)
female ab. *lanceolata* Shipp - extreme development
of upperside spotting.

Photos: Natural Image/Alec S. Harmer (unless otherwise stated).

observed in a Somerset colony, and a female of this aberration was taken by me for breeding. The F_1 generation were typical and in the F_2 generation ab. *obsoleta* Tutt. appeared. The male illustrated emerged in the F_3 generation.

Interestingly, there are differing opinions as to whether or not *radiata* and *obsoleta* are controlled by a single gene, with the latter the more extreme expression of *radiata*. The breeding experiences of Nigel Potter and Les Young in the early 1960s demonstrated that the two were not genetically separate (Potter & Young, 1965). However, Tom Robertson's experiments previously described led to him to conclude that the two aberrations were distinct from one another and that in their heterozygous state both appear to be incomplete recessives, referable to *partimauroradiata* (Robertson, 1995a). The original female from which he bred his *radiata + pallidula* was of this form. My limited experience of breeding *obsoleta* accords with his findings. One possible explanation for these different conclusions could be that *obsoleta* is controlled by modifying genes whose extent of control over its expression varies significantly between different populations. Careful breeding of either of these aberrant forms from different localities would help clarify the situation. Any female displaying incomplete banding of the hindwing certainly would be worth breeding through to at least the F_2 generation.

The homoeotic female depicted has the pattern of the underside of the forewing reproduced on both hindwings. She was one of two specimens displaying bilateral underside homoeosis that emerged in October 1984 from a brood of eleven females from a typical female I took at Portland. In view of the fact that there were two in the same brood and homoeosis has been recorded previously in this species from this locality, the condition may well have some heritable basis.

In some summers it is not unusual to find the normally bright copper of the forewings in the Small Copper heavily suffused in the later generations (Plate 15, figs 1, 2). The male ab. *fuscae* Robson in the photograph was taken by me in September at Corfe, Dorset in the hot summer of 1989. This aberration is almost certain to be environmentally controlled.

Common Blue, *Polyommatus icarus* (Rottemburg) (page 88, a)

I AM INDEBTED to Richard Revels for supplying the original stock from which I bred the striking aberration of ab. *radiata* Courvoisier featured. He started with a slightly rayed female to which he later introduced unrelated stock bred by Les Young containing the genes for ab. *elongata* Tutt and ab. *extensa* Tutt, and through selective breeding has produced these most extreme forms.

It is understood that the variable extent of development of *radiata* amongst individuals is controlled by the interaction of a complex of genes which work together to produce a cumulative effect. This is an example of multifactorial or polygenic inheritance, in which this cumulative effect can be intensified through selective breeding. Evidence that this aberration is not purely controlled by a simple recessive is demonstrated by the fact that occasionally typical specimens and gradations occur amongst the progeny from a pairing between two *radiata* (Revels, 1998a).

These breeding experiments help to confirm that, in this species at least, spot development is heritable. It is probable that the character can also be induced through environmental influences. As far as I am aware, very little research has been carried out on these forms in this subgenus, most likely because uncertainty of success results in an understandable reluctance on the part of collectors to breed from such rare and treasured specimens.

The Chalk Hill Blue, *Lysandra coridon* (Poda) (page 88, c - f)

Iₙ ᴄᴇʀᴛᴀɪɴ populations of the Chalk Hill Blue, most noticeably those in Dorset, two beautiful but rare aberrations known as ab. *fowleri* South and ab. *ultrafowleri* Bright & Leeds are occasionally found (Plate 21, figs 1, 2; Plate 22, figs 1, 2, 5, 6). In *fowleri*, the normal black marginal borders to the upperside of the forewings have been replaced with white and contain no dots or pupils. The hindwings have the normal ocelli with perhaps less black than usual. In *ultrafowleri*, the borders of all wings are devoid of these dots, the border on the inner side of the forewings being either very narrow or mere shading. Very often the normal blue colouring of the male is replaced with a beautiful pale silvery blue in both of these aberrations. The same recessive gene is responsible for both *fowleri* and *ultrafowleri*, with the degree of expression controlled by modifying genes, with full expression culminating in *ultrafowleri*.

The female *fowleri* on page 88 was taken at Portland in 1984 and is the only one I have encountered in this sex. She had particularly well-marked forewings but the resulting females in the F₂ generation were not so distinct, having a brown suffusion overlaying the white lunules. This suffusion also affected some of the males to a lesser degree. This variable gene expression in the female probably explains why *fowleri* is far more often seen in males than females in the field, even allowing for the less conspicuous nature of the latter sex, particularly during ovipositing. The experiences of both other collectors and myself put this ratio somewhere between eight and ten males to every female. The aberration appears in equal ratios in both sexes when bred. The male ab. *ultrafowleri-margino* Bright & Leeds (page 88, d) emerged in the F₃ generation.

Once not uncommon in Wiltshire, and in the Chilterns in Buckinghamshire, but now seldom encountered, the beautiful all blue form of ab. *tithonus* Meigen is found only in the female and is an extremely rare example of a single recessive gene which is not only sex-linked (being attached to the Z chromosome in the female) but also sex-limited. The specimen of this aberration and that of ab. *tithonus + fowleri* were bred from stock that originated from Ralph Tubbs, from a female taken in 1967. This latter aberration, involving two recessive genes, is a dihybrid cross with modified Mendelian ratios owing to sex linkage being involved.

The Adonis Blue, *Lysandra bellargus* (Rottemburg) (page 88, b; page 89, a)

Iᴛ ɪs apparent that environmental conditions can affect underside spotting in this species. In the marvellous summer of 1983, the Adonis Blue at Corfe had an excellent second brood and was to be found not only on the hillsides but all over the lucerne field in the photograph on page 30. Many of the specimens were below average size and several males were taken by me with the forewing submedian spots elongating inwards, referable to ab. *disco-juncta* Courvoisier; the best specimen is depicted. Interestingly, several examples tending towards obsolescence of the forewing spotting were also taken at the same time. My experience of this colony is that it has never shown any such comparatively extreme tendencies before or since that summer, in the twenty-five years or more that I have been visiting it. Some elongation and duplication ('dribbling') of the forewing underside submedian spots are frequently met with in this species and have been found to be heritable, most probably on a multifactorial basis (Robertson & Young, 1982). This article also includes several current theories regarding the determination of wing-pattern, and their possible application to the Adonis Blue with respect to the particular spot development just mentioned.

In the exceptional hot summers of 1975 and 1976, corresponding aberrations to these striated forms occurred amongst the Chalk Hill Blue population on Portland. Aberrations ranging from ab. *discoelongata* Bright & Leeds to ab. *antistriata* Bright & Leeds were not uncommon. In 1975, Don took a female ab. *ultraradiata* Bright & Leeds (*Aberrations of British Butterflies*: Plate 11, fig. 10) at Portland, a locality rarely producing such extreme forms. In the circumstances it would be reasonable to assume that all these forms are mainly environmentally controlled.

In passing, I would just clarify the differences between the various 'rayed' underside forms which are a recurring theme in the Lycaenidae. They can be categorized as being either 'striated' or 'radiated'. In the former, the development of the median spots is in an inward direction towards the base of the wing. In the latter, the development is outwards towards the marginal chevrons. Just to confuse matters slightly, the renowned Victorian lepidopterist J. W. Tutt was obstinately inconsistent in his descriptions: his *striata* in the Common Blue is the exact opposite to his *striata* in the Chalk Hill Blue.

The mixed gynandromorph shown is most unusual inasmuch as the left hindwing is completely female and reduced to about half normal size. The loss of a Z chromosome would have taken place after the first cell division, most likely during development of the third thoracic segment.

The Red Admiral, *Vanessa atalanta* (L.)
The Painted Lady, *Cynthia cardui* (L.) (page 89, e)

JUST how much the external environment can affect wing pattern development is strikingly illustrated in the two butterflies shown here. The specimens are from Karl Bailey's temperature experiments and represent both ends of the spectrum of thermal shock treatment. His research has indicated that in the Red Admiral, ab. *klemensiewiczi* Schille can be induced using high temperature shock at the early pupal stage. Conversely, cold temperature treatment at the same stage can produce ab. *elymi* Rambur in the Painted Lady. Of particular interest is the pattern of similarity which exists between two aberrations in different species.

The Pearl-bordered Fritillary, *Boloria euphrosyne* (Denis & Schiffermüller) (page 89, c, d)

THE two aberrant specimens illustrate clearly two recurring themes represented right across the Nymphalidae. In the first photograph, the normal rich fulvous ground colour is replaced by pale ochreous and is ab. *albinea* Lambillion. It is most likely determined by a simple recessive gene as the aberration recurs in the same locality; I have taken two there within half an hour of each other. In other years, the same woods produced an even more whitish form, and from stock from the same locality, I have bred the straw-coloured ab. *stramineus* Frohawk. It is reasonable to assume that a gradation exists between these two named forms. Parallel aberrations are shown in the Small Pearl-bordered Fritillary on Plate 46, figs 3, 4, and in the Silver-washed Fritillary on Plate 54, figs 1, 2. Although around half a dozen male ab. *cifkai* Silbernagel have been taken, I am not aware of any females having been seen or captured.

The second photograph illustrates the phenomenon known as melanism which is responsible for some of the most dramatic of all aberrations occurring in Lepidoptera. It was mentioned earlier that the deposition of melanin can be influenced by extremes of temperature and, sometimes, the genetic make-up of the individual concerned. The melanic female in the photograph is ab. *edna* Lobb and was taken in May 1988 (at the same locality as the original female aberration captured by Mr J. Lobb, some thirty-six years earlier). From my diary notes, most of the first three weeks of May 1988 were dry and warm, with daytime temperatures no lower than 20°C (usually 22°-23°C). The recurrence of the aberration in the same locality does point towards there being some heritable basis involved, possibly requiring the unseasonably warm temperatures during the critical period around pupation to trigger the necessary gene reaction. Perhaps in this early emerging species, pupating as it does when frosts are still likely, it is the low - as opposed to high - temperatures that normally should be considered as being the more frequent cause for the appearance of aberrations.

The Silver-washed Fritillary, *Argynnis paphia* (L.) (page 89, f)

THE four male specimens featured are the result of cold temperature treatment. Although collectors have differing - often very strong - views regarding temperature experimentation, one of several benefits to be derived from this practice is that it often reveals the spectrum of gradation in development (often following a sequential progression or morphocline) that sometimes exists between what may at first appear to be quite separate and distinct aberrational forms.

Earlier, in discussing external environmental influence, the comparative abundance of melanic aberrations in this particular species in certain years was mentioned. A study of the daily temperatures for June and July for those years undertaken by Rupert Barrington (1989) showed a clear correlation between spells of abnormally high maximum temperatures around the estimated time of pupation and the occurrence of extreme melanics in this species. An average daily shade temperature of 19°C for June was established from data collected and a significant departure from average was regarded as being 21°C and above. The highest temperature recorded (36°C on 25th June 1976) was exceptionally high in relation to the other temperatures which for the most part remained below 30°C. The daily minimum temperatures were examined and assumed not to have played any part as nothing exceptional was recorded. Remarking on the great difference in temperatures for producing aberrations in the wild, as opposed to those required to create them artificially (40°-45°C in the Standfuss experiment), Rupert Barrington offers the explanation that exposed larvae and pupae are capable of absorbing the sun's radiated heat to the extent that their internal temperatures are far in excess of those externally; a phenomenon found in other cold-blooded animals. He cites Keith Porter as having recorded the internal temperature of larvae of the Marsh Fritillary as being over 35°C due to radiation when the air temperature was little above 0°C. The logical explanation, therefore, for the higher temperatures needed to bring about these forms artificially is the fact that unlike in the natural state, no solar radiation factor is involved; the internal temperature of the organism can only achieve equilibrium with the external temperature. It is perhaps no coincidence that our early Fritillary larvae are black - such coloration is most effective in absorbing solar radiation at a time of the year when air temperatures are still low. The resulting increase in the internal temperature of the larva enables essential metabolic processes such as digestion, to function properly.

From what has been said, it would obviously pay the collector to keep a weather eye open and to note any incidents of abnormal temperatures coinciding with critical developmental stages. Similarly, any locality with topographical features such as low lying areas, hollows etc. which may be susceptible to frost or, alternatively, act as sun traps, is worth investigating.

The Gatekeeper, *Pyronia tithonus britanniae* Verity (page 90, a)

THE photograph shows a female of an extremely rare aberration found in this common butterfly in which the borders of the forewings are considerably widened to beyond the apical eyespot and the hindwings almost completely black-brown. Richard Revels has bred ab. *lugens* Oberthür from a Cambridgeshire female, demonstrating that it is controlled by a simple dominant gene.

The Meadow Brown, *Maniola jurtina* (L.)(page 89, b; page 90, b)

VERY rarely, the apical eye spot of the forewing may be entirely absent in this species, being described as ab. *anommata* Verity (Plate 79, fig. 1). The male featured in the photograph was captured on the North Downs in Surrey. I am not aware of this aberration having been bred but I would suspect that the gene responsible is essentially recessive in character but subject to some modification. The bilateral gynandromorph illustrated was a fortunate capture for Richard Revels from a local Bedfordshire wood.

The Ringlet, *Aphantopus hyperantus* (L.)(page 90, c - f)

AN EXAMPLE of the part that chance and good fortune often play in collecting and breeding is illustrated by the following episode. One particular favourite aberration which has constantly eluded me until recently is the rare and beautiful ab. *lanceolata* Shipp (Plate 83) which is a simple recessive. In 1995, at the invitation of my friends John and Eileen Quinn, I joined them to spend a few days collecting in a private wood in Sussex. The owner had very kindly granted us access and the purpose of the trip was to secure a female Purple Emperor for breeding. While waiting for one to be enticed down from the treetops by John's ingenious methods, I turned my attentions to a small colony of Ringlets that happened to be in the same clearing. I had only examined a few when I was rewarded with the capture of a most extreme female *lanceolata* (see photograph). Several more were taken that afternoon and the following morning and some of these were kept for breeding. Fortunately, the Ringlet is an easy species to rear, accepting a range of grasses in captivity. Having succeeded in obtaining *lanceolata*, I then wanted to fulfil a long-standing ambition which was to cross it with ab. *arete* Müller, a not uncommon aberration in many colonies of this butterfly. I was content to wait until the following season before securing a specimen of this aberration. However, a week later I went to Portland primarily to look over the Chalk Hill Blues, but shortly after arriving netted a female *arete*! I have always been aware of the small Ringlet colony in this most unlikely habitat but had never given it close attention in the past. She was set up to lay and unexpectedly, *arete* appeared in the F_1 generation in the following year. This, however, was not evidence that the gene was dominant, as was later proved by further breeding. The isolated nature and size of this island population meant that the male she had paired with was heterozygous for the same gene.

The hoped for pairing between *lanceolata* and *arete* was eventually achieved but the results, although admittedly pleasing, were somewhat less than expected. Of the 122 imagines that emerged in the F_2 generation in 1998, I obtained the following results: 84 typical; 24 arete; 12 *lanceolata*; and 2 *lanceolata* + *arete* (both females). This was not quite the expected 9 : 3 : 3 : 1 Mendelian ratio for a dihybrid cross (Diagram 5). I had hoped, too, that the extreme nature of this particular *lanceolata* gene might have resulted in a far more spectacular aberration.

This cross has previously been achieved by Major-General C. G. Lipscomb (*Aberrations of British Butterflies*: Plate 35, figs 5, 6) and Major A. E. Collier (1960). Collier's specimens are in the National Collection and include several similar to the female illustrated and others with just one or two very reduced normal or lanceolate spots remaining, chiefly on the forewings. I would make a personal observation here. Rather interestingly, Collier, in the write-up of his results, mentions that: 'The proportions of the different phenotypes this year confirmed again the simple recessive character of *lanceolata*, and, at the same time, quite fortuitously and misleadingly, I think, pointed at the same condition in *arete*, which is generally accepted as a multiple factor inheritance.' I suspect that the reference to multiple factor inheritance alludes to the opinion expressed by Ford (1945). My albeit limited breeding experience of *arete* - confined to my Portland female - is that the gene responsible acts as a simple recessive. I have had no gradated forms emerge, even after the introduction of the unrelated *lanceolata* stock. The suggestion put forward earlier in reference to *obsoleta* and *radiata* in the Small Copper could equally apply here to explain these different findings i.e. that in different Ringlet populations in which the *arete* gene occurs, its expression is subject to modification by other genes present, the amount of control varying from colony to colony. Further breeding is being undertaken in order to study the genetics of this intriguing cross.

Ironically, the female in the last illustration resulted naturally from stock released in the garden the previous year, consisting of individuals judged by me as not sufficiently extreme enough from which to breed! She has quite the most marked upperside spot development that I have seen so far, exceeding anything produced by my selective breeding efforts.

Chapter Six

Tips for Success

ALTHOUGH the foregoing has given an insight into the genetics responsible for a few of our aberrations, there is obviously very much more still awaiting discovery. The scope and potential for doing so is considerable with a total of 3,538 aberrations listed in *Colour Identification Guide to Butterflies of the British Isles*, with more described since its publication. This figure is slightly reduced as it includes those species prohibited from being collected under The Wildlife and Countryside Act 1981. The list of protected species is reviewed every five years and collectors need to ensure that they are conversant with the current status of any particular species. In addition, they should also adhere to the guidance laid down in *A Code of Insect Collecting* prepared by the Joint Committee for the Conservation of British Insects. Abiding by it should not be a problem, however, given the infrequent occurrence of aberrations in the wild.

For reasons that should be self-evident, butterflies are not usually selected for professional genetic research; other Orders, particularly the Diptera, being far more suitable for laboratory study. Indeed, much of what is known about genetics is through the tremendous amount of research carried out on the fruit fly (*Drosophila* species). Our knowledge so far of the genetics of butterflies is derived principally from the efforts of amateur lepidopterists and no doubt this particular field of the science will continue to be regarded as being very much their own domain. Thus, the collector has freedom of access to a wealth of genetic opportunity.

Throughout this book reference has been made to the rarity of aberrations in nature and it follows that in the circumstances most should be made of any opportunity that presents itself. With this view in mind, in this closing chapter I have put together some thoughts covering the practical aspects of breeding butterflies, using the Chalk Hill Blue by way of example, although many of the points mentioned are fundamental to the breeding of other species. If more detailed information is required regarding a particular species, several useful publications are given in the bibliography.

Before contemplating breeding any aberration, several matters need consideration, not least the likelihood of the aberration being heritable (the foregoing might have provided guidance in this respect). Equally important, too, are the chances of bringing the species through at least two generations; some butterflies can be extremely difficult to breed in captivity. Where the intention is to concentrate on a particular species, prior breeding experience would greatly increase the overall chances of success with the aberration itself. Of course, this is not always possible as aberrations have the engaging habit of turning up quite unexpectedly in any species. Other matters to be considered include the availability of foodplant, and being available at the critical moments of emergence, pairing etc.

Much as we may wish it otherwise, not every captured aberration on inspection turns out to be a flawless specimen. In the event of this situation arising, the collector is immediately faced with a difficult choice: either to risk damaging the specimen in the attempt to breed from it in the hope of obtaining further, possibly even more extreme, aberrations, or simply to accept good fortune and take it for the cabinet. Damaged or worn aberrations present no such problems. Almost certainly, females in this condition would probably have paired and can automatically be consigned to the breeding cage. Often though, an aberration turns out to be a worn male, suitable only for admiring briefly before being released. Yet, with a little planning and preparation, even this unpromising situation may be successfully turned to the breeder's advantage.

By way of illustration, I mentioned earlier that in the Chalk Hill Blue, ab. *fowleri* South is more often encountered in the males. In the light of this knowledge it would be worth maintaining some typical stock in captivity (under natural conditions so that emergence times coincide) in anticipation of a virgin female being required. Such foresight has paid dividends for me. There is another benefit to be gained from this practice. Inbreeding for the purposes of obtaining aberrations can have a debilitating effect upon stock viability. The resulting specimens are often undersized, exhibit a reluctance to pair, low fecundity, or generally suffer mortality in the later developmental stages. Bred typical stock can be used to outcross with the aberrant strain to maintain vigour. The aberration, although temporarily suppressed, will reappear in subsequent generations.

A plentiful supply of foodplant is an essential requirement. There needs to be a sufficient quantity available, not only to cater for the number of larvae expected and to preclude any need for overcrowding which might otherwise increase the likelihood of disease, but also to enable different genetic lines to be maintained separately. Some plants have developed chemical defence mechanisms to protect themselves from the unwelcome attentions of larvae, slugs, snails and other creatures. The production of hydrogen cyanide as a defence strategy by White Clover *(Trifolium repens)* is a classic example. It is therefore a wise precaution periodically to move livestock on to fresh plants before this phenomenon occurs. In addition, in my experience, Horseshoe Vetch, *Hippocrepis comosa*, the foodplant of the Chalk Hill Blue, rarely recovers from overgrazing. A calcareous-loving plant with a very deep tap-root, enabling the plant to survive arid conditions, it should not be dug up from the wild. Apart from it being illegal to do so, the breeder runs the risk of introducing any wild ova or larvae already on the foodplants into his genetic lines, so jeopardizing the integrity of his results. Instead, plants can be raised from stem cuttings or collected seeds. Wild flower nurseries can supply seeds and young plants. The plants will take several years to get established and a considerable number of them will be needed if several broods of the butterfly are going to be raised. Under cultivation, in the sheltered conditions of a flower pot, Horseshoe Vetch will often flourish and become leggy and bushy, unlike plants exposed to their natural environment. While this does provide more food for the larvae, it can attract powdery mildew. It is wise to keep the plant as close to its natural state as possible by periodic trimming.

The Chalk Hill Blue thrives best on growing foodplant but it needs to be borne in mind that in the artificial environment of a netted container conditions are very different from those in the wild. Netting of plants, while keeping out predators, does affect the circulation of air around the plant. The build up of frass created by the larvae combined with humid still air create ideal conditions for unwelcome fungal development, predisposing the larvae to bacterial and viral infection. Plants are also susceptible to frost when grown in flower pots and so need to be protected in an unheated greenhouse, cold frame or sheltered car port. The plants should be kept reasonably dry during the winter and are best left uncovered to minimise the chances of aphid infestation. In the spring, to protect the newly hatched larvae during their first few instars from predators, I confine them in small, very fine net sleeves placed over a stem, plugged at each end with cotton wool and carefully tied off, to avoid crushing the stem. If there is absolute confidence that the potted plant is free of predators, this precaution can be dispensed with. When it is certain that the rest of the plant is free of predators, the larvae can safely be released on to the plant. At this stage, a few ants (not wood ants!) can be introduced as they seem to have a beneficial effect on the larvae. The young larvae will need to be protected from heavy rain and this aspect will need careful monitoring through all stages of development. Watering plants is best done sparingly and from underneath. It is best to avoid too many larvae on any plant especially in the later instars. The leaves are small and the plant will be defoliated in a matter of days and it is a time-consuming business to have to move them on continually, besides running the risk of disturbing and damaging larvae preparing for pupation. Regular checks over a period of several days will be necessary to ensure that all larvae have been cleared from the plant. They have a habit of getting right down in amongst the roots and continue to appear in a supposedly cleared pot - like rabbits from a magician's hat. If not removed, they will eat the plant down to the bare stems, with the consequences previously mentioned. A slight depression in the soil on top of the pot, covered over by a flat piece of stone, provides a suitable site for pupation. When the pupae have hardened they can be transferred to a plastic container for safety.

One major ongoing problem that continually has to be overcome when rearing larvae on growing foodplant is the presence of predators. The amazing ability of slugs, earwigs, woodlice, beetles, spiders, aphids etc. to survive all attempts intended to ensure their eradication is an education in itself. Constant vigilance and carrying out these preliminary precautions are the secrets to ensuring their potential to cause utter devastation is eliminated. All soil used for potting up foodplants should be sterilized or be of a suitable proprietary type to avoid the introduction of pests. Any drainage holes in containers should be covered sufficiently to deny them access. I use a water-proof epoxy resin adhesive to secure plastic, fly-screen mesh for this purpose. The size of the mesh squares can be reduced by overlaying two pieces. It is essential that a thorough inspection of foodplants is carried out before they are planted up. Admittedly, it is difficult to remove completely all potential predators from some foodplants and although submerging the foodplant in a bucket of water or water butt for a day does help eliminate the adult stages of predators to some degree, it cannot be relied on totally and is not so effective against the other stages. Again, vigilance is paramount and should include periodic checks after dark by torchlight, most predators being nocturnal.

Flowers provided for nectar also need to be rigorously examined for unwelcome guests, before being introduced and again on their removal, as butterflies will often deposit their eggs on them. Cotton wool pads soaked in sugar solution and used to augment the nectar supply should be removed overnight as they attract predators. It is a wise precaution to collect up the ova every day and to overwinter them in a small, airtight plastic container in a cool garage. To make this task easier, I find it useful to pack sterilized (a few minutes in a hot oven) sphagnum moss around the base of the foodplant. The females will oviposit quite happily on this. Although The Chalk Hill Blue is single-brooded, ova have been known to hatch a few weeks after being laid. Therefore, frequent checks should be made during this critical period.

Any netting used to cover containers should be fine enough to keep out the smallest hymenopterous intruder. Whatever is used for securing the netting, needs to remain taut enough to keep out predators, and to be regularly inspected.

Finally, it is well to remember not all predators are small. Speaking from personal experience, cats with their strange perversity will insist on choosing netted tubs and flower pots upon which to curl up and go to sleep. They are also drawn to fluttering butterflies in cages.

ADDENDA AND NOTES

ADDENDA AND NOTES

PART THREE:

The Colour Plates

Specimens are numbered from left to right going down the page.

When a life study is placed at the side of a set specimen this shows upper and underside of the same insect.

When the figures are placed down the centre of the plate upper and underside of the same specimen are shown with the set specimen above and a life-study below except where indicated.

A reference to a specimen being within a particular collection relates to its location at the time the paintings were originally completed.

All butterflies are reproduced natural size.

PLATE 1

The Chequered Skipper
Carterocephalus palaemon (Pallas, 1771)

FIGS 1&2
Northamptonshire
18.5.1948
G. E. Hyde

male ab. *melicertes* Schultz

FIGS 3&4
Near Wansford, Cambs.
24.5.1956
G. E. Hyde

female ab. *lutea-excessa* Tutt

PLATE 2

The Silver-spotted Skipper
Hesperia comma (Linneaus, 1758)

FIGS 1&2
Box Hill, Surrey
August 1954
A. D. A. Russwurm

female - enlarged median spots

The Large Skipper
Ochlodes venata faunus (Turati, 1905)

FIGS 3&4
New Forest, Hants.
24.7.1951
A. D. A. Russwurm

male ab. *obscura* Tutt

The Grizzled Skipper
Pyrgus malvae (Linnaeus, 1758)

FIGS 5&6
Frimley, Surrey
20.5.1951
A. D. A. Russwurm

female ab. *taras* Bergsträsser

PLATE 3

The Swallowtail
Papilio machaon britannicus Seitz, 1907

FIGS 1&2
Heigham Sound, Norfolk
31.5.1950
A. D. A. Russwurm

male - reduced yellow markings due to expansion of
sub-marginal forewing band

PLATE 4

The Swallowtail

Papilio machaon britannicus Seitz, 1907

Bred at Chelmsford, Essex
(larva from Norfolk Broads
ex. L. W. Newman)
24.4.1930
H. C. Ferrier
(H. J. Turner Coll.)

male ab. *obscura* Frohawk

PLATE 5

The Clouded Yellow
Colias croceus (Geoffroy, 1785)

FIGS 1&2
Swanage, Dorset
23.9.1960
R. Hayward
(R. W. Watson Coll.)

female ab. *hyerensis* Strand

FIGS 3&4
Seaford, Sussex
20.8.1949
A. D. A. Russwurm

female ab. *pseudomas* Cockerell

PLATE 6

The Brimstone
Gonepteryx rhamni rhamni (Linnaeus, 1758)

FIGS 1&2
Bred from ova
Hunts.
July 1928
G. E. Hyde

Mixed gynandromorph

FIGS 3&4
Bred at Surbiton, Surrey
from larva taken on East Coast
1920
M. Summers
(H. J. Turner Coll.)

male ab. *nigrescens* Hechler

PLATE 7

The Green-veined White
Pieris napi britannica Müller & Kautz, 1939
Pieris napi thomsoni Warren, 1968

FIG. 1
Donegal, Ireland
July 1940
J. Shepherd

ssp. *britannica* Müller & Kautz
female ab. *interjuncta* Cabeau

FIG. 2
Co. Clare, Ireland
July 1914
L. W. Newman

ssp. *britannica* Müller & Kautz
female ab. *fasciata* Kautz

FIG. 3
Caithness, Scotland
5.6.1928
Rev. J. N. Marcon

ssp. *thomsoni* Warren
female ab. *continua* Bryk

FIG. 4
Bred ex. Donegal, Ireland
July 1940
H. Wood

ssp. *britannica* Müller & Kautz
female ab. *flavicans* Müller

FIG. 5
Bred ex. Donegal, Ireland
July 1949
H. J. Turner

ssp. *britannica* Müller & Kautz
female ab. *sulphurea* Schöyen
+ *fasciata* Kautz

FIG. 6
Bred ex. Donegal, Ireland
July 1947
H. J. Turner

ssp. *britannica* Müller & Kautz
male ab. *sulphurea* Schöyen
+ *conjuncta* Lempke

FIG. 7
Caithness, Scotland
May 1936
L. W. Newman

ssp. *thomsoni* Warren
male - heavy scaling of hindwing veins

FIG. 8
Donegal, Ireland
July 1919
H. W. Head

ssp. *britannica* Müller & Kautz
male - heavy scaling of hindwing veins

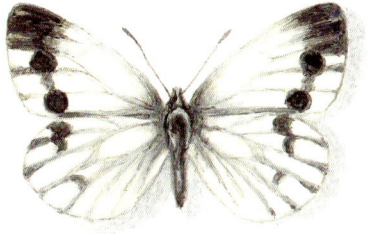

PLATE 8

The Orange-tip
Anthocharis cardamines britannica (Verity, 1908)

FIG. 1
Tenbury, Worcs.
11.5.1917
(H. J. Turner Coll.)

Bilateral gynandromorph

FIG. 2
Castor, Northants.
E. A. Bright
(H. J. Turner Coll.)

Mixed gynandromorph

FIGS 3&4
Chiddingfold, Surrey
8.5.1954
S. G. Castle Russell
(H. J. Turner Coll.)

male ab. *aureoflavescens* Cockerell

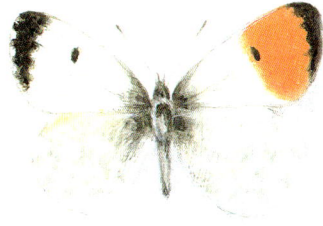

PLATE 9

The Orange-tip
Anthocharis cardamines britannica (Verity, 1908)

Cobham, Kent
19.5.1974
A. S. Harmer

male ab. *antiquincunx* Bryk

FIG. 3
Lymington, Hants.
15.5.1980
A. S. Harmer

male ab. *reducta* Masowicz
+ *striata* Pionneau + *crassipuncta* Mezger

PLATE 10

The Brown Hairstreak
Thecla betulae (Linnaeus, 1758)

FIG. 1
Bred ex. ova
Purton, Wilts.
9.7.1978
A. S. Harmer

male ab. *spinosae* Gerhard

FIG. 2
Bred ex. ova
Balls Cross, Sussex
10.8.1977
A. S. Harmer

female ab. *lata* Tutt

FIG. 3
Bred ex. ova
Purton, Wilts.
9.7.1978
A. S. Harmer

female ab. *restricta-lineata* Tutt

PLATE 11

The Purple Hairstreak
Neozephyrus quercus (Linnaeus, 1758)

FIGS 1&2
Bred New Forest, Hants.
July 1965
H. G. M. Middleton

male ab. *violacea* Niepelt

FIGS 3&4
Bred New Forest, Hants.
July 1965
H. G. M. Middleton

female ab. *caerulescens* Lempke

FIGS 5&6
Bred New Forest, Hants.
July 1965
H. G. M. Middleton

female ab. *obsoleta* Tutt

PLATE 12

The Purple Hairstreak
Neozephyrus quercus (Linnaeus, 1758)

Bred ex. larvae beaten from
Ashtead Wood, Surrey
July 1964
S. F. Imber

FIG. 1
female - transitional to ab. *latefasciata* Courvoisier

FIG. 2
female ab. *latefasciata* Courvoisier

FIG. 3
male ab. *infraobscura* Goodson

PLATE 13

The Small Copper
Lycaena phlaeas eleus (Fabricius, 1798)

FIGS 1&2
Mitcham, Surrey
2.5.1943
L. A. Sabine

male ab. *schmidtii* Gerhardt

FIGS 3&4
Hod Hill, Dorset
20.9.1959
A. D. A. Russwurm

female ab. *cuprinus* Peyerimhoff

FIGS 5&6
Watford, Hertfordshire
4.8.1960
L. D. Young

female ab. *melanophlaeas* Villiers & Guenée

FIGS 7&8
Chipstead, Surrey
21.8.1941
L. A. Sabine

male ab. *supra-radiata* Oberthür

PLATE 14

The Small Copper
Lycaena phlaeas eleus (Fabricius, 1798)

FIG. 1
Hod Hill, Dorset
20.9.1959
A. D. A. Russwurm

female ab. *radiata* Tutt

FIG. 2
Bred Surrey
July 1962
L. D. Young

female ab. *obsoleta* Tutt

FIG. 3
Bred Surrey
July 1964
L. D. Young

female ab. *fuscata* Tutt
+ *obsoleta* Tutt

FIG. 4
Bred Surrey
July 1964
L. D. Young

female ab. *extensa-conjuncta* Tutt

FIG. 5
South Devon
20.9.1971
Capt. A. P. Gainsford

female ab. *extensa* Tutt
+ *infra-radiata* Tutt

FIG. 6
Bred ex. male Surrey and female
ex. Somerset
July 1964
L. D. Young

female ab. *anticentrijuncta* Leeds

FIG. 7
Bred ex. Somerset F$_2$
October 1963
L. D. Young

female - homoeosis
ab. *inaequalis* Leeds

FIG. 8
Bred Surrey
27.8.1962
L. D. Young

female ab. *bipunctata* Tutt

PLATE 15

The Small Copper
Lycaena phlaeas eleus (Fabricius, 1798)

FIGS 1&2
Dorset
2.9.1962
H. J. Turner

male ab. *fuscae* Robson
+ *extensa* Tutt + transitional to *obsoleta* Tutt

FIGS 3&4
Harting Down, Sussex
14.8.1954
N. B. Potter
(L. D. Young Coll.)

female upperside ab. *bipunctata* Tutt
underside ab. *antico-radiata* Derenne

FIGS 5&6
Wembury Point, Devon
10.10.1969
Capt. A. P. Gainsford
(B.M.N.H.)

male ab. *berviniensis* Smith

PLATE 16

The Silver-studded Blue
Plebejus argus argus (Linnaeus, 1758)
Plebejus argus caernensis Thompson, 1937

FIG. 1
Pirbright, Surrey
July 1939
B. H. Smith

ssp. *argus* (Linnaeus)
female - intersex

FIG. 2
Pirbright, Surrey
July 1939
B. H. Smith

ssp. *argus* (Linnaeus)
female - intersex

FIG. 3
Chobham, Surrey
July 1917
S. G. Castle Russell

ssp. *argus* (Linnaeus)
female - intersex

FIG. 4
Chobham, Surrey
July 1917
S. G. Castle Russell

ssp. *argus* (Linnaeus)
male ab. nov.

FIG. 5
North Wales
27.6.1952
H. J. Turner

ssp. *caernensis* Thompson
typical female

FIG. 6
North Wales
27.6.1952
H. J. Turner

ssp. *caernensis* Thompson
typical female

FIG. 7
Portland, Dorset
20.8.71
A. S. Harmer

ssp. *argus* (Linnaeus)
female ab. *flavuslunulatus* Tutt

FIG. 8
North Wales
27.6.1952
H. J. Turner

ssp. *caernensis* Thompson
typical female

PLATE 17

The Silver-studded Blue
Plebejus argus argus (Linnaeus, 1758)

FIG. 1
New Forest, Hants.
1.7.1971
A. D. A. Russwurm

male ab. *privata* Courvoisier

FIG. 2
Worth Matravers, Dorset
5.7.1952
H. J. Turner

male ab. nov.
hindwings near to ab. *costo-retrojuncta*
Courvoisier

FIG. 3
Worth Matravers, Dorset
5.7.1952
H. J. Turner

female ab. nov.

FIG. 4
New Forest, Hants.
13.7.1964
A. D. A. Russwurm

female ab. *juncta* Tutt

FIG. 5
New Forest, Hants.
1.7.1971
A. D. A. Russwurm

female ab. *caeca* Grund

FIG. 6
New Forest, Hants.
July 1960
A. D. A. Russwurm

female ab. *obsoleta-juncta* Tutt

PLATE 18

The Brown Argus
Aricia agestis ([Denis & Schiffermüller], 1775)

The Northern Brown Argus
Aricia artaxerxes artaxerxes (Fabricius, 1793)

The Castle Eden Argus
Aricia artaxerxes salmacis (Stephens, 1831)

FIG. 1
Dorset
29.5.1949
H. J. Turner

A. agestis ([D.& S.])
male ab. *pallidior* Oberthür

FIG. 2
Witherslack, Cumbria
July 1925
T. M. Blackman

ssp. *salmacis* (Stephens)
male ab. *pallidior* Oberthür

FIG. 3
Galashiels, Borders,
Scotland
14.7.1904

ssp. *artaxerxes* (Fabricius)
male ab. *snelleni* Ter Haar

FIG. 4
Kincardineshire, Scotland
August 1928
G. E. Hartley

ssp. *artaxerxes* (Fabricius)
male ab. *snelleni* Ter Haar + *unicolor*
Lempke

FIG. 5
Ashford, Kent
19.7.1912
H. Wood

A. agestis ([D.& S.])
female ab. nov.

FIG. 6
Arnside, Lancashire
25.7.1971
H. G. M. Middleton

ssp. *salmacis* (Stephens)
female ab. *postico-obsoleta* Tutt

FIG. 7
Hod Hill, Dorset
16.6.1962
J. F. Kimber

A. agestis ([D.& S.])
male ab. *deleta* Cockerell

FIG. 8
Abbots Wood, Sussex
19.8.1922
L. F. Hammond
(H. J. Turner Coll.)

A. agestis ([D.& S.])
female ab. *nigropunctata* Tutt

PLATE 19

The Common Blue

Polyommatus icarus icarus (Rottemburg, 1775)
Polyommatus icarus mariscolore (Kane, 1893)

FIG. 1
Co. Galway, Ireland
24.6.1928
L. A. Sabine

ssp. *mariscolore* (Kane)
Bilateral gynandromorph

FIG. 2
Co. Mayo, Ireland
1.7.1926
S. B. Hodgson

ssp. *mariscolore* (Kane)
Bilateral gynandromorph

FIG. 3
Co. Galway, Ireland
24.7.1927
L. A. Sabine

ssp. *mariscolore* (Kane)
Mixed gynandromorph

FIG. 4
Co. Sligo, Ireland
2.7.1952
Rev. J. N. Marcon

ssp. *mariscolore* (Kane)
Mixed gynandromorph

FIG. 5
Worth Matravers, Dorset
22.8.1971
A. S. Harmer

ssp. *icarus* (Rottemburg)
female ab. *apicata-supracaerulea* Tutt

FIG. 6
Kincardineshire, Scotland
1915
A. Horne

ssp. *icarus* (Rottemburg)
female - well-developed lunules

FIG. 7
Co. Sligo, Ireland
1.7.1952
Rev. J. N. Marcon

ssp. *mariscolore* (Kane)
female - well-developed lunules

FIG. 8
Ashbury
June 1942
B. H. Smith
(R. W. Watson Coll.)

ssp. *icarus* (Rottemburg)
female ab. *rufina* Oberthür

PLATE 20

The Common Blue

Polyommatus icarus icarus (Rottemburg, 1775)

FIG. 1
Surrey
1935
A. T. Mitchell

male ab. *antico-obsoleta* Tutt
+ *postico-striata* Tutt

FIG. 2
Sussex
25.5.1935
Rev. J. N. Marcon

male ab. *antico-striata* Tutt
+ *subobsoleta* Tutt

FIG. 3
Huntingdonshire
1.6.1933
H. A. Leeds

male ab. *parvipuncta* Tutt
+ *albescens* Tutt + *barnumi* Dujardin

FIG. 4
Huntingdonshire
25.5.1934
H. A. Leeds

male ab. *antico-obsoleta* Tutt

FIG. 5
Chilterns, Bucks.
18.8.1928
H. A. Leeds

male ab. *radiata* Courvoisier

FIG. 6
Ashford, Kent
17.8.1934
H. Wood

female ab. *antico-striata* Tutt

PLATE 21

The Chalk Hill Blue
Lysandra coridon (Poda, 1761)

FIGS 1&2
Worth Matravers, Dorset
August 1959
A. D. A. Russwurm

male ab. *fowleri* South

FIGS 3&4
Worth Matravers, Dorset
August 1917
H. J. Turner

male ab. *cinnameus* Bright & Leeds

FIGS 5&6
Shoreham, Sussex
3.8.1947
Rev. J. N. Marcon
(H. J. Turner Coll.)

male ab. *melaina* Tutt

FIGS 7&8
Shoreham, Sussex
8.8.1936
Rev. J. N. Marcon
(H. J. Turner Coll.)

male ab. *supramelaina* Bright & Leeds

PLATE 22

The Chalk Hill Blue
Lysandra coridon (Poda, 1761)

FIGS 1&2
Badbury Rings, Dorset
4.8.1941
F. S. Reeves

male ab. *ultrafowleri* Bright & Leeds
underside ab. *alba* Bright & Leeds + *obsoleta* Tutt

FIGS 3&4
Worth Matravers, Dorset
August 1960
A. D. A. Russwurm

male ab. *punctata* Tutt

FIGS 5&6
Worth Matravers, Dorset
11.8.1946
(ex. S. G. Castle Russell Coll.)

female ab. *fowleri* South

FIG. 7&8
Worth Matravers, Dorset
12.8.1950
(ex. S. G. Castle Russell Coll.)

female ab. *punctata* Tutt

PLATE 23

The Chalk Hill Blue
Lysandra coridon (Poda, 1761)

FIG. 1
Standlynch Downs, Wilts.
1941
H. Haynes

Mixed gynandromorph

FIG. 2
Shawford, Hants.
9.8.1951
R. W. Watson

Mixed gynandromorph

FIG. 3
Royston, Herts.
August 1954
A. D. A. Russwurm

female ab. *ultraalbocrenata* Bright & Leeds

FIG. 4
Royston, Herts.
August 1953
A. D. A. Russwurm

female ab. *semisyngrapha-subaurantia* Tutt

FIG. 5
Royston, Herts.
August 1953
A. D. A. Russwurm

female ab. *semisyngrapha-subaurantia* Tutt

FIG. 6
Royston, Herts.
August 1955
A. D. A. Russwurm

female ab. *semisyngrapha-subaurantia* Tutt

FIG. 7
Salisbury District, Wilts.
August 1955
H. J. Turner

female ab. *tithonus* Meigen

FIG. 8
Salisbury District, Wilts.
August 1947
H. J. Turner

female ab. *pertithonus* Tutt

PLATE 24

The Chalk Hill Blue
Lysandra coridon (Poda, 1761)

FIG. 1
Dorset
August 1950
K. W. Self

male ab. *obsoleta* Tutt
+ *transiens* Bright & Leeds

FIG. 2
Royston, Herts.
August 1957
A. D. A. Russwurm

male ab. *obsoleta* Tutt

FIG. 3
Corfe Castle, Dorset
26.7.1946
K. W. Self
(R. W. Watson Coll.)

male ab. *extrema* Bright & Leeds

FIG. 4
Folkestone, Kent
July 1952
K. W. Self

male ab. *radiata* Bright & Leeds

FIG. 5
Hertfordshire
13.8.1923
H. A. Leeds
(H. J. Turner Coll.)

female ab. *obsoleta* Tutt

FIG. 6
Amberley, Sussex
1.8.1936
W. G. Pether

female ab. *antistriata* Bright & Leeds

FIG. 7
Shoreham, Sussex
6.8.1955
R. E. Stockley
(R. W. Watson Coll.)

female ab. *antiextrema* Bright & Leeds
+ *postalba* Bright & Leeds
+ *limbojuncta* Courvoisier

FIG. 8
Shoreham, Sussex
5.8.1938
R. L. E. Ford
(H. J. Turner Coll.)

female ab. *alba-radiata* Bright & Leeds

PLATE 25

The Adonis Blue
Lysandra bellargus (Rottemburg, 1775)

FIGS 1&2
typical male

FIGS 3&4
typical female

PLATE 26

The Adonis Blue
Lysandra bellargus (Rottemburg, 1775)

FIG. 1
Hod Hill, Dorset
4.6.1950
I. G. Farwell

female ab. *marginata* Tutt

FIG. 2
St. Catherine's Hill, Hants.
2.6.1950
I. G. Farwell

female ab. nov.

FIG. 3
Folkestone, Kent
29.8.1931
H. Wood
(H. J. Turner Coll.)

Mixed gynandromorph

FIG. 4
Folkestone, Kent
4.9.1928
H. Wood
(H. J. Turner Coll.)

Mixed gynandromorph

FIG. 5
Folkestone, Kent
29.8.1932
Rev. J. N. Marcon

Bilateral gynandromorph

FIG. 6
Hod Hill, Dorset
31.5.1936
I. G. Farwell

female - transitional to ab. *caerulescens*
Oberthür

FIG. 7
Hod Hill, Dorset
5.6.1961
A. D. A. Russwurm

female ab. *semiceronus* Tutt

FIG. 8
Hod Hill, Dorset
5.6.1961
A. D. A. Russwurm

female ab. *semiceronus* Tutt

PLATE 27

The Adonis Blue
Lysandra bellargus (Rottemburg, 1775)

FIG. 1
Hod Hill, Dorset
30.5.1954
I. G. Farwell

male ab. *krodeli* Gillmer + *detersa* Verity

FIG. 2
Dorset
June 1950
H. J. Turner

male ab. *krodeli* Gillmer + *detersa* Verity

FIG. 3
Sussex
30.8.1940
Rev. J. N. Marcon

male - transitional to
ab. *disco-elongata* Courvoisier

FIG. 4
Hod Hill, Dorset
September 1959
A. D. A. Russwurm

male ab. *krodeli* Gillmer

FIG. 5
Hod Hill, Dorset
6.9.1959
A. D. A. Russwurm

female ab. *krodeli* Gillmer

FIG. 6
Dorset
May 1949
H. J. Turner

male ab. *detersa* Verity + *conjuncta* Tutt +
hindwings near to *cinnides* Staudinger

FIG. 7
Sussex
7.6.1940
Rev. J. N. Marcon
(H. J. Turner Coll.)

female ab. *striata* Tutt

FIG. 8
Sussex
9.9.1938
Rev. J. N. Marcon

male ab. *conjuncta* Tutt

PLATE 28

The Holly Blue
Celastrina argiolus britanna (Verity, 1919)

FIG. 1
Seaford, Sussex
May 1955
A. D. A. Russwurm

typical male - spring generation

FIG. 2
Sutton Coldfield, Warwickshire
26.4.1912
G. B. Oliver
(H. J. Turner Coll.)

Bilateral gynandromorph

FIG. 3
Bred New Forest, Hants.
1940
H. J. Turner

typical female - spring generation

FIG. 4
Seaford, Sussex
May 1955
A. D. A. Russwurm

typical female - spring generation

FIG. 5
North Kent
July 1941
H. J. Turner

female ab. *lilacina-suffusa* Tutt

FIG. 6
New Forest, Hants.
August 1954
H. J. Turner

typical female - summer generation

FIG. 7
New Forest, Hants.
1.5.1946
H. J. Turner

ab. *paucipuncta* Courvoisier

FIG. 8
Parracombe Common, Devon
August 1945
A. D. Turner
(H. J. Turner Coll.)

male ab. nov.

PLATE 29

The Large Blue
Maculinea arion eutyphron (Fruhstorfer, 1915)

FIGS 1&2
Bude, Cornwall
15.7.1905

typical male

FIGS 3&4
Millook, Cornwall
18.7.1909
A. A. Smith

typical female

PLATE 30

The Duke of Burgundy Fritillary
Hamaeris lucina (Linnaeus, 1758)

FIGS 1&2
New Forest, Hants.
18.5.1966
H. G. M. Middleton

male ab. *semibrunnea* Osthelder

FIGS 3&4
Bred ex. Hod Hill, Dorset
May 1941
H. J. Turner

Bilateral gynandromorph

FIGS 5&6
Crundale, Kent
June 1925
P. Richards

female ab. *albomaculata* Blachier

PLATE 31

The White Admiral
Limenitis camilla (Linnaeus, 1764)

FIGS 1&2
New Forest, Hants.
19.7.1965
A. D. A. Russwurm

male ab. *obliterae* Robson & Gardner

FIG. 3
New Forest, Hants.
22.7.1965
A. D. A. Russwurm

male ab. *obliterae* Robson & Gardner

PLATE 32

The White Admiral
Limenitis camilla (Linnaeus, 1764)

FIGS 1&2
New Forest, Hants.
24.7.1965
I. G. Farwell

male ab. *nigrina* Weymer

FIG. 3
New Forest, Hants.
12.7.1941
I. G. Farwell

female ab. *nigrina* Weymer

PLATE 33

The Purple Emperor
Apatura iris (Linnaeus, 1758)

FIGS 1&2
typical male

FIG. 3
typical female

PLATE 34

The Purple Emperor
Apatura iris (Linnaeus, 1758)

FIGS 1&2
New Forest, Hants.
23.7.1900
Miller

male ab. *iolata* Cabeau

FIG. 3
Bred ex. Northamptonshire
6.7.1900
E. A. Rogers

female ab. *iolata* Cabeau

PLATE 35

The Purple Emperor
Apatura iris (Linnaeus, 1758)

FIG. 1
Chattenden Wood, Kent
about 1870
(ex. Sir Vauncey Harpur Crewe Coll.)
(ex. Webb Coll.)
(ex. H. D. Bessemer Coll.)
(B.M.N.H.)

male ab. *lugenda* Cabeau

FIG. 2
no data
(ex. P. M. Bright Coll.)

male ab. *lugenda* Cabeau

FIG. 3
Near Pulborough, Sussex
bred from wild larva
26.6.1943
A. J. Wightman
(ex. H. D. Bessemer Coll.)
(B.M.N.H.)

female ab. *lugenda* Cabeau

PLATE 36

The Purple Emperor
Apatura iris (Linnaeus, 1758)

FIGS 1&2
Wiltshire,
25.7.1960
I. R. P. Heslop

male upper and underside
ab. *sorbioduni* Heslop

FIG. 3
Chattenden Wood, Kent
July 1878
T. W. Wood
(ex. E. L. Bolton Coll.)
(R. W. Watson Coll.)

male ab. *lugenda* Cabeau

PLATE 37

The Painted Lady
Cynthia cardui (Linnaeus, 1758)

FIGS 1&2
Chilterns, Bucks.
29.7.1922
G. B. Oliver

female ab. *priameis* Schultz

PLATE 38

The Painted Lady
Cynthia cardui (Linnaeus, 1758)

Folkestone, Kent
1938
H. J. Turner

female ab. *priameis* Schultz

FIGS 3&4
Colchester, Essex
1917
(H. J. Turner Coll.)

male ab. *varini* Meilhan

PLATE 39

The Small Tortoiseshell
Aglais urticae (Linnaeus, 1758)

FIGS 1&2
Bred Brockenhurst, Hants.
ex. Hod Hill, Dorset
26.6.1961
A. D. A. Russwurm

male ab. *semiichnusoides* Pronin

FIGS 3&4
Pignal Inclosure,
New Forest, Hants.
21.7.1965
A. D. A. Russwurm

male ab. *semiichnusoides* Pronin

PLATE 40

The Small Tortoiseshell
Aglais urticae (Linnaeus, 1758)

FIGS 1&2
Bred Brockenhurst, Hants.
June 1956
J. F. Kimber

male ab. *semiichnusoides* Pronin

FIGS 3&4
Ringwood, Hants.
30.9.1947
D. Watson
(ex. E. L. Bolton Coll.)
(R. W. Watson Coll.)

female - transitional to ab. *conjuncta* Neuberg

PLATE 41

The Large Tortoiseshell
Nymphalis polychloros (Linnaeus, 1758)

FIGS 1&2
New Forest, Hants.
1902
Simmons

One of six aberrations (two deformed) bred from
a brood of about eighty larvae found on sallow
near Lady Cross.
(R. W. Watson Coll.)

female ab. *testudo* Esper

PLATE 42

The Peacock
Inachis io (Linnaeus, 1758)

FIG. 1
Bred Boldre, Hants.
17.7.1948
I. G. Farwell

male ab. *fulva* Oudemans

FIGS 2&3
Bred Brockenhurst, Hants.
3.8.1960
A. D. A. Russwurm

female ab. *exoculata* Weymer

PLATE 43

The Comma
Polygonia c-album (Linnaeus, 1758)

FIGS 1&2
Near Oxford
1.7.1930
L. W. Newman

male ab. *obscura* Closs

FIGS 3&4
Brockenhurst, Hants.
22.9.1964
A. D. A. Russwurm

male ab. *obscura* Closs

PLATE 44

The Comma
Polygonia c-album (Linnaeus, 1758)

FIGS 1&2
Forest of Dean, Glos.
27.7.1934
G. B. Oliver
(H. J. Turner Coll.)

male ab. *suffusa* Frohawk - extreme form

FIGS 3&4
Forest of Dean, Glos.
27.7.1934
G. B. Oliver

male ab. *reichstettensis* Fettig

FIGS 5&6
Forest of Dean, Glos.
7.8.1934
G. B. Oliver

male ab. *reichstettensis* Fettig

PLATE 45

The Small Pearl-bordered Fritillary
Boloria selene selene ([Denis & Schiffermüller], 1775)

FIGS 1&2
New Forest, Hants.
26.6.1932
J. R. Freeman
(H. J. Turner Coll.)

male ab. *obsoleta* Curtis

FIGS 3&4
New Forest, Hants.
4.6.1942
H. J. Turner

male ab. *halflantsi* Cabeau

FIGS 5&6
East Sussex
June 1918
V. Penn
(H. J. Turner Coll.)

male - melanic ab. - wings black except
for light marginal chevrons

PLATE 46

The Small Pearl-bordered Fritillary
Boloria selene selene ([Denis & Schiffermüller], 1775)

FIGS 1&2
Roe Inclosure,
New Forest, Hants.
16.6.1964
A. D. A. Russwurm

male - melanic ab.

FIGS 3&4
Copthorne, West Sussex
1.6.1944
(A. S. Harmer Coll.)

male ab. nov. - pale straw ground colour

FIGS 5&6
Polegate, East Sussex
1.6.1936
(A. S. Harmer Coll.)

male ab. *nigricans* Oberthür

FIGS 7&8
New Forest, Hants.
July 1931
(A. S. Harmer Coll.)

male ab. *vanescens* Cabeau

PLATE 47

The Pearl-bordered Fritillary
Boloria euphrosyne (Linnaeus, 1758)

FIGS 1&2
Ashstead, Surrey
May 1953
A. D. A. Russwurm

male ab. nov. - postmedian spots enlarged

FIGS 3&4
New Forest, Hants.
5.6.1965
A. D. A. Russwurm

female ab. *conducta* Nordstrom

FIGS 5&6
Pignal Inclosure,
New Forest, Hants.
7.6.1964
A. D. A. Russwurm

female - melanic ab.

FIG. 7
New Forest, Hants.
2.6.1971
A. S. Harmer

male - transitional to ab. *dorensis* Real

FIG. 8
Pignal Inclosure,
New Forest, Hants.
14.5.1971
A. D. A. Russwurm

male ab. *tatrica* Aigner

PLATE 48

The Pearl-bordered Fritillary
Boloria euphrosyne (Linnaeus, 1758)

FIGS 1&2
Abbots Wood, Sussex
1897
(ex. H. D. Bessemer Coll.)
(B.M.N.H.)

male ab. nov. - markings almost absent

FIGS 3&4
Ulverstone, Lancs.
June
H. Murray
(H. J. Turner Coll.)

female ab. nov.

FIGS 5&6
New Forest, Hants.
June 1948
R. W. Watson

male ab. *edna* Lobb

PLATE 49

The High Brown Fritillary
Argynnis adippe vulgoadippe Verity, 1929

FIG. 1
New Forest, Hants.
July 1965
H. J. Turner

male ab. nov.

FIG. 2
New Forest, Hants.
27.6.1941
H. J. Turner

male - transitional to ab. *margareta* Stephan

FIG. 3
Arnside, Lancs.
6.8.1971
H. G. M. Middleton

female ab. nov.

PLATE 50

The High Brown Fritillary
Argynnis adippe vulgoadippe Verity, 1929

FIGS 1&2
Sussex
30.6.1945
Rev. J. N. Marcon
(H. J. Turner Coll.)

male ab. *bronzus* Frohawk

FIGS 3&4
Berkshire
17.7.1935
Rev. J. N. Marcon

male ab. *callisto* Cabeau

PLATE 51

The Dark Green Fritillary
Argynnis aglaja aglaja (Linnaeus, 1758)

FIGS 1&2
Langdon Hole, Kent
16.7.1900

male ab. *wimani* Holmgren

FIGS 3&4
Box Hill, Surrey
10.7.1929
G. H. Strickland
(H. J. Turner Coll.)

male upperside ab. *cadmeis* Lempke
underside ab. nov.

PLATE 52

The Dark Green Fritillary
Argynnis aglaja aglaja (Linnaeus, 1758)

FIGS 1&2
North Kent
1915
L. W. Newman

male ab. *cadmeis* Lempke

FIGS 3&4
Charterhouse, Somerset
28.7.1964
B. J. Withers

male ab. nov.

PLATE 53

The Dark Green Fritillary
Argynnis aglaja aglaja (Linnaeus, 1758)

FIGS 1&2
Mendips, Somerset
21.7.1974
A. S. Harmer

male ab. *viridiatra* Strand

FIG. 3
Great Ridge, Wilts.
21.7.1978
A. S. Harmer

female ab. nov.

PLATE 54

The Silver-washed Fritillary
Argynnis paphia (Linnaeus, 1758)

FIGS 1&2
New Forest, Hants.
24.7.1913
Butterworth

male ab. *cifkai* Silbernagel

FIG. 3
New Forest, Hants.
July 1919
F. Gulliver
(R. W. Watson Coll.)

male ab. *ocellata* Frings

PLATE 55

The Silver-washed Fritillary
Argynnis paphia (Linnaeus, 1758)

FIG. 1
New Forest, Hants.
16.7.1919
D. C. Johnstone

male ab. *ocellata* Frings

FIGS 2&3
New Forest, Hants.
July 1932
T. Beale

female ab. *ocellata* Frings

PLATE 56

The Silver-washed Fritillary
Argynnis paphia (Linnaeus, 1758)

FIG. 1
New Forest, Hants.
21.7.1941
I. G. Farwell

male ab. *confluens* Spuler

FIG. 2
Fritham, New Forest, Hants.
6.7.1956
I. G. Farwell

female ab. *ocellata* Frings

FIG. 3
New Forest, Hants.
20.7.1958
H. J. Turner

female ab. *ocellata* Frings

PLATE 57

The Silver-washed Fritillary
Argynnis paphia (Linnaeus, 1758)

FIGS 1&2
New Forest, Hants.
22.7.1941
Rev. J. N. Marcon

female ab. *ocellata* Frings

FIGS 3&4
New Forest, Hants.
July 1919
A. H. Campbell
(H. J. Turner Coll.)

female ab. *nigrizina* Frohawk

PLATE 58

The Silver-washed Fritillary
Argynnis paphia (Linnaeus, 1758)

FIG. 1
New Forest, Hants.
1897
C. Gulliver
(A. S. Harmer Coll.)

male ab. *ocellata* Frings

FIGS 2&3
New Forest, Hants.
17.7.1942
V. R. Burkhardt
(H. J. Turner Coll.)

female ab. *nigricans* Cosmovici

PLATE 59

The Silver-washed Fritillary
Argynnis paphia (Linnaeus, 1758)

FIGS 1&2
New Forest, Hants.
6.7.1942
J. Tetley

Mixed gynandromorph

FIG. 3
New Forest, Hants.
17.7.1963
A. D. A. Russwurm

female - somatic mosaic

PLATE 60

The Silver-washed Fritillary
Argynnis paphia (Linnaeus, 1758)

New Forest, Hants.
24.7.1922
W. G. Nash

Bilateral gynandromorph
right side - form *valesina* Esper

FIG. 3
Pignal Inclosure,
New Forest, Hants.
16.7.1939
I. G. Farwell

Bilateral gynandromorph

PLATE 61

The Marsh Fritillary
Euphydryas aurinia (Rottemburg, 1775)

FIGS 1&2
Hod Hill, Dorset
1.6.1967
A. D. A. Russwurm

male ab. *melanoleuca* Cabeau

FIGS 3&4
Bred ex. Hod Hill, Dorset
1.6.1966
A. D. A. Russwurm

female ab. *epimolpadia* Reverdin

PLATE 62

The Marsh Fritillary
Euphydryas aurinia (Rottemburg, 1775)

FIGS 1&2
North Devon
29.5.1942
N. A. Watkins
(B.M.N.H.)

male - transitional to ab. *melanoleuca* Cabeau

FIGS 3&4
ex. Hod Hill, Dorset
J. Shepherd

female 26.6.1936

ab. *bicolor* Wehrti

FIGS 5&6
ex. Hod Hill, Dorset
J. Shepherd

male 24.5.1936

ab. *bicolor* Wehrti

PLATE 63

The Glanville Fritillary
Melitaea cinxia (Linnaeus, 1758)

FIGS 1&2
Bred ex. Isle of Wight
1962
H. J. Turner

female ab. *uhryki* Aigner

FIGS 3&4
Bred ex. Isle of Wight
7.6.1929
G. Nobbs
(H. J. Turner Coll.)

female ab. *horvathi* Aigner

PLATE 64

The Glanville Fritillary
Melitaea cinxia (Linnaeus, 1758)

FIGS 1&2
Bred ex. Brook, Isle of Wight
21.5.1961
I. G. Farwell

male ab. *horvathi* Aigner

FIGS 3&4
Bred Portmore, ex. Isle of Wight
19.5.1961
I. G. Farwell

female ab. nov.

FIGS 5&6
Bred Brockenhurst, ex. Isle of Wight
19.6.1971
A. D. A. Russwurm

male underside ab. *expuncta* Cabeau
upperside ab. nov.

PLATE 65

The Glanville Fritillary
Melitaea cinxia (Linnaeus, 1758)

FIG. 1
Bred ex. Isle of Wight
1945
H. J. Turner

male ab. *wittei* Geest

FIG. 2
Bred ex. Isle of Wight
1945
H. J. Turner

female ab. *wittei* Geest

FIG. 3
Bred ex. Isle of Wight
1961
H. J. Turner

female ab. *wittei* Geest

PLATE 66

The Heath Fritillary
Melitaea athalia (Rottemburg, 1775)

FIGS 1&2
Sussex
16.6.1952
Rev. J. N. Marcon

male ab. *nigromarginata* Lempke

FIGS 3&4
North Kent
7.7.1927
L. W. Newman

female - transitional to ab. *cymothoë* Bertolini

FIGS 5&6
Blean Woods, Kent
1.7.1936
J. Shepherd
(H. J. Turner Coll.)

female ab. *latonigena* Spuler

PLATE 67

The Heath Fritillary
Melitaea athalia (Rottemburg, 1775)

FIGS 1&2
Blean Woods, Kent
June 1936
H. J. Turner

male ab. *corythallia* Hübner

FIGS 3&4
Church Wood, Blean, Kent
24.6.1973
A. S. Harmer

male ab. *corythallia* Hübner

FIGS 5&6
Sussex
16.6.1952
H. J. Turner

female ab. *cymothoë* Bertolini

FIGS 7&8
Hadleigh, Essex
July 1948
(H. J. Turner Coll.)

male underside ab. *tetramelana* Cabeau

PLATE 68

The Speckled Wood
Pararge aegeria tircis (Godart, 1821)

FIGS 1&2
New Forest, Hants.
20.5.1966
A. D. A. Russwurm

female ab. *parviocellata* Lempke

FIGS 3&4
New Forest, Hants.
5.8.1966
A. D. A. Russwurm

female ab. *schmidti* Dioszeghy
+ *postico-excessa* Lempke + *punctata* Gussich

PLATE 69

The Wall
Lasiommata megera (Linnaeus, 1767)

PLATE 70

The Scotch Argus
Erebia aethiops aethiops (Esper, 1777)

FIGS 1&2
Arnside, Westmorland
3.8.1971
H. G. M. Middleton

female ab. *infasciata* Warren

FIGS 3&4
Arnside, Westmorland
2.8.1967
A. D. A. Russwurm

female ab. *infasciata* Warren + *ochracea* Mosley

FIGS 5&6
Arnside, Westmorland
4.8.1970
A. D. A. Russwurm

Bilateral gynandromorph

PLATE 71

The Marbled White
Melanargia galathea serena Verity, 1913

FIGS 1&2
Bred Sussex
July 1952
Major A. E. Collier

female ab. *mosleyi* Oberthür

FIGS 3&4
Bred Sussex
July 1952
Major A. E. Collier

male ab. *mosleyi* Oberthür

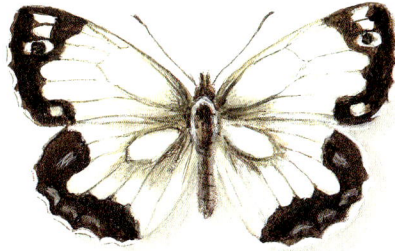

PLATE 72

The Marbled White
Melanargia galathea serena Verity, 1913

FIGS 1&2
Portland, Dorset
1.8.1980
T. M. Melling

female ab. *nigricans* Culot

FIG. 3
Whiteparish, Wilts.
21.7.1972
A. S. Harmer

male ab. *semigalene* Stauder

PLATE 73

The Grayling
Hipparchia semele semele (Linnaeus, 1758)

FIGS 1&2
Portland, Dorset
12.8.1973
H. G. M. Middleton

male ab. *monocellata* Lempke + *postcaeca* Schawerda

FIGS 3&4
Portland, Dorset
28.7.1973
A. S. Harmer

female ab. *monocellata* Lempke

PLATE 74

The Grayling
Hipparchia semele semele (Linnaeus, 1758)

FIG. 1
New Forest, Hants.
12.8.1965
A. D. A. Russwurm

male ab. *jubaris* Fruhstorfer

FIG. 2
New Forest, Hants.
5.8.1966
A. D. A. Russwurm

male - pathological

FIG. 3
New Forest, Hants.
31.7.1965
A. D. A. Russwurm

male ab. *monocellata* Lempke + *postcaeca* Schawerda

PLATE 75

The Grayling
Hipparchia semele semele (Linnaeus, 1758)

FIG. 1
Aberdovey, Merioneth
16.8.1922
A. Owen
(B.M.N.H.)

female ab. *holonops* Brouwer

FIG. 2
Folkestone, Kent
August 1935
L. W. Newman

female ab. *thyone* Schultz + *postcaeca* Schawerda

FIG. 3
Sussex
3.8.1938
J. Tetley
(B.M.N.H.)

female ab. *addenda* Tutt

PLATE 76

The Gatekeeper
Pyronia tithonus britanniae (Verity, 1915)

FIGS 1&2
New Forest, Hants.
30.7.1956
A. D. A. Russwurm

male - pathological

FIGS 3&4
New Forest, Hants.
July 1950
A. D. A. Russwurm

male ab. *seminigra* Rocci

FIGS 5&6
New Forest, Hants.
8.7.1956
A. D. A. Russwurm

male ab. *infra-unicolora* Lempke

PLATE 77

The Gatekeeper
Pyronia tithonus britanniae (Verity, 1915)

FIGS 1&2
Cork
August 1929
(ex. Greer Coll.)

female ab. *subalbida* Verity + *excessa* Tutt

FIGS 3&4
Brockenhurst, Hants.
July 1960
A. D. A. Russwurm

female - pathological

FIGS 5&6
Burrington, North Devon
20.8.1945
E. S. Scarlet

female ab. *crassiexcessa* Leeds - extreme lanceolate form

PLATE 78

The Meadow Brown
Maniola jurtina insularis Thomson, 1969

FIGS 1&2
New Forest, Hants.
9.7.1957
A. D. A. Russwurm

male ab. *radiata* Frohawk

FIG. 3
New Forest, Hants.
12.7.1960
A. D. A. Russwurm

male ab. *alba* Blackie

FIG. 4
Near Petersfield, Hants.
7.8.1946
A. D. A. Russwurm

male ab. *transformis* Leeds

PLATE 79

The Meadow Brown
Maniola jurtina insularis Thomson, 1969

FIG. 1
New Forest, Hants.
28.7.1962
A. D. A. Russwurm

male ab. *anommata* Verity

FIG. 2
New Forest, Hants.
8.8.1962
A. D. A. Russwurm

female ab. *postmultifidis* Lipscomb

FIG. 3
Pignal Inclosure, New Forest, Hants.
7.7.1969
A. D. A. Russwurm

female ab. *postmultifidus* Lipscomb

FIG. 4
Surrey
22.7.1955
R. E. Stockley

female ab. nov.

PLATE 80

The Small Heath
Coenonympha pamphilus pamphilus (Linnaeus, 1758)

FIGS 1&2
Hod Hill, Dorset
July 1962
H. J. Turner

female ab. nov. - transitional to ab. *alba* Prüffer

FIGS 3&4
Ben Lawers, Perthshire
1.7.1973
H. G. M. Middleton

male ab. *caeca* Oberthür

FIGS 5&6
Arnside, Westmorland
23.6.1968
H. G. M. Middleton

male ab. *bipupillata* Cosmovici + *obliquajuncta* Leeds

FIGS 7&8
New Forest, Hants.
July 1952
H. J. Turner

male ab. *partimtransformis* Bright & Leeds

PLATE 81

The Large Heath
Coenonympha tullia davus (Fabricius, 1777)

FIGS 1&2
Witherslack, Westmorland
June 1933
G. Watkinson

female ab. *lanceolata* Arkle

FIGS 3&4
Shropshire
26.6.1949
A. Eckford

male ab. *addenda* Lempke

FIGS 5&6
Witherslack, Westmorland
July 1932
G. Watkinson

male ab. *lanceolata* Arkle

FIGS 7&8
Witherslack, Westmorland
26.6.1922
G. Watkinson

male ab. *lanceolata* Arkle

PLATE 82

The Large Heath
Coenonympha tullia davus (Fabricius, 1777)
Coenonympha tullia polydama (Haworth, 1803)
Coenonympha tullia scotica Staudinger, 1901

FIG. 1
Delamere Forest, Cheshire
June 1915
L. W. Newman

ssp. *davus* (Fabricius)
male ab. *lanceolata* Arkle

FIG. 2
Co. Galway, Ireland
June 1930
L. A. Sabine

ssp. *polydama* (Haworth)
male - reduced ocelli

FIG. 3
Meathop Moss, Westmorland
3.7.1969
A. D. A. Russwurm

ssp. *davus* (Fabricius)
female ab. *impupillata* Lempke

FIG. 4
Goathland, Yorkshire
7.7.1951
A. D. A. Russwurm

ssp. *polydama* (Howarth)
male ab. nov.

FIG. 5
Whixall Moss, Shropshire.
July 1951
R. W. Watson

ssp. *davus* (Fabricius)
male ab. *cockaynei* Hopkins

FIG. 6
Whixall Moss, Shropshire.
July 1951
R. W. Watson

ssp. *davus* (Fabricius)
male ab. *cockaynei* Hopkins

FIG. 7
Isle of Arran
July 1913
W. Smith

ssp. *scotica* Staudinger
typical male

FIG. 8
Isle of Arran
July 1913
W. Smith

ssp. *scotica* Staudinger
typical male

PLATE 83

The Ringlet
Aphantopus hyperantus (Linnaeus, 1758)

FIGS 1&2
New Forest, Hants.
July 1956
A. D. A. Russwurm

female ab. *lanceolata* Shipp

FIG. 3
Fritham
New Forest, Hants.
July 1958
A. D. A. Russwurm

male ab. *lanceolata* Shipp

FIG. 4
Fritham
New Forest, Hants.
July 1958
C. R. Haxby

female ab. *lanceolata* Shipp

PLATE 84

The Ringlet
Aphantopus hyperantus (Linnaeus, 1758)

FIGS 1&2
Fritham, New Forest, Hants.
July 1958
C. R. Haxby
(A. D. A. Russwurm Coll.)

male - pathological

FIG. 3
New Forest, Hants.
July 1956
A. D. A. Russwurm

male ab. nov. - hindwing ocelli with white pupils well-developed

FIG. 4
Chipstead, Surrey
July 1949
A. D. A. Russwurm

male ab. *arete* Müller

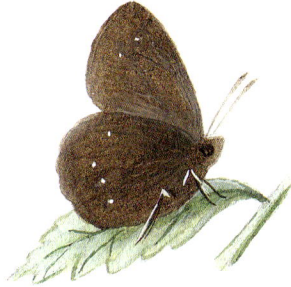

BIBLIOGRAPHY

REFERENCES AND FURTHER READING

ACKWORTH, B., 1947. *Butterfly Miracles and Mysteries.* Eyre & Spottiswoode, London. **[Illustrated by A. D. A. Russwurm]**

ACKWORTH, B., 1955. *Bird and Butterfly Mysteries.* Eyre & Spottiswoode, London. **[Illustrated by A. D. A. Russwurm]**

BAILEY, K. E. J., 1998. A new pupal and imaginal aberration of the marsh fritillary *Eurodryas aurinia* Rott. (Lep.: Nymphalidae). *Br. J. Ent. Nat. Hist.,* **11**: 7-11, pl. 1, figs 5-8.

BARRINGTON, R. D. G., 1984. Notes on Variation in a North Dorset Colony of the Meadow Brown, *Maniola jurtina* L. *Entomologist's Rec. J. Var.,* **96**: 259-263, 6 figs.

BARRINGTON, R. D. G., 1989. Melanic aberrations of the Silver-washed Fritillary (*Argynnis paphia* L.) in North Dorset in 1986, and the relevance of temperature on the occurrence of such forms in the wild. *Entomologist's Rec. J. Var.,* **101**: 267-274, 4 figs.

BARRINGTON, R. D. G., 1992a. A breeding experiment with *Maniola jurtina* L. (meadow brown butterfly) ab. *postmultifidus* Lipscomb. *Br. J. Ent. Nat. Hist.,* **5**: 155-157, 8 figs.

BARRINGTON, R. D. G., 1994a. Breeding *Maniola jurtina* L. ab. *addenda* Mo[u]sley (Lep.: Satyridae). *Entomologist's Rec. J. Var.,* **106**: 13-15, 6 figs.

BARRINGTON, R. D. G., 1999a. A breeding experiment with *Maniola jurtina* L. ab. *fracta* Zweig[e]lt (Lep.: Satyridae). *Br. J. Ent. Nat. Hist.,* **11**: 149-151, 8 figs.

BARRINGTON, R. D. G., 1999c. The genetics of the melanic ab. *nigricans* Culot of *Melanargia galathea* L. (Lep. Nymphalidae: Satyrinae). *Entomologist's Rec. J. Var.,* **111**: 269-271, pls B, C.

BARRINGTON, R. D. G. & YOUNG, L. D., 1990. A major breeding experiment with two aberrations of *Polyommatus icarus* Rott., the common blue butterfly. *Br. J. Ent. Nat. Hist.,* **3**: 3-10, pl. 1.

BATESON, W., 1894. *Materials for the Study of Variation,* p. 85.

BATESON, W., 1900. *Proc. zool. Soc., Lond.,* p. 268.

BECCALONI, G. W., 1988. A possibly unique bilateral gynandromorph of the white admiral butterfly, *Ladoga camilla* L. *Entomologist's Rec. J. Var.,* **100**: 102-104, 1 fig.

BOLTON, E. L., 1950. An albinic aberration of *Thymelicus acteon* [ab. *alba*]. *Entomologist,* **83**: 63.

BOLTON, E. L., 1951. [Record of exhibit at Annual Exhibition 1950 - *Thymelicus acteon* ab. *alba* Bolton]. *Proc. Trans. S. Lond. ent. nat. Hist. Soc.,* **1950-51**: 20, pl. I, fig. 6.

BRADLEY, J. D., 1998. *Checklist of Lepidoptera recorded from the British Isles.* D. J. & M. J. Bradley, Fordingbridge.

BRETHERTON, R. F., 1963. Inter-sex and other Aberrations of the Silver-studded Blue (*Plebejus argus* L. (*aegon* Schiff.)) in North-west Surrey, 1963. *Entomologist's Rec. J. Var.,* **75**: 277-278.

BRIGHT, P. M. & LEEDS, H. A., 1938. *A Monograph of the British Aberrations of the Chalk-hill Blue Butterfly Lysandra coridon (Poda, 1761).* Richmond Hill Printing Works, Bournemouth.

COCKAYNE, E. A., 1922. *Intersexual forms* of Plebeius argus *L.* (aegon *Schiff.*). *Trans. ent. Soc. Lond.*, 225-239, pls V-IX.

COCKAYNE, E. A., 1926a. Homoeosis and heteromorphosis in insects. *Trans. R. ent. Soc. Lond.*, **78**: 203-229, pls 61-64.

COCKAYNE, E. A., 1926b. Intersexes in the Lycaenidae. *Proc. Trans. S. Lond. ent. nat. Hist. Soc.*, **1926-27**: 24-29.

COCKAYNE, E. A., 1935. The Origin of Gynandromorphs in the Lepidoptera from Binucleate Ova. *Trans. R. ent. Soc Lond.*, **83**: 509-521.

COCKAYNE, E. A., 1938. The Genetics of Sex in Lepidoptera. *Biol. Rev.*, **13**: 107-132.

COLLIER, MAJOR A. E., 1955. A note on *Agapetes (Melanargia) galathea* L. ab. *aperta* Rebel. *Entomologist's Rec. J. Var.*, **67**: 1-5, pl. 1.

COLLIER, MAJOR A. E., 1956b. A Successful Rearing of *Lysandra coridon* Poda ab. *syngrapha* Kef. *Entomologist's Rec. J. Var.*, **68**: 281-282.

COLLIER, MAJOR A. E., 1958. The Genetics of *Lysandra coridon* Poda ab. *syngrapha* Kef. *Entomologist's Rec. J. Var.*, **70**: 278-279.

COLLIER, MAJOR A. E., 1959b. *Lysandra coridon* Poda ab. *syngrapha* Kef. a sex limited character. *Entomologist's Rec. J. Var.*, **71**: 284.

COLLIER, MAJOR A. E., 1960. *Aphantopus hyperantus* L. ab. *lanceolata* Shipp + *arete* Müll. *Entomologist's Rec. J. Var.*, **72**: 260-261.

DOWDESWELL, W. H., 1981. *The Life of the Meadow Brown*. Heinemann Educational Books, London.

EMMET, A. M. & HEATH, J. (Eds.), 1989. *The Moths and Butterflies of Great Britain and Ireland Vol. 7, Part 1* The Butterflies. Harley Books, Colchester.

FORD, E. B., 1945. *Butterflies*. New Naturalist Series, Collins, London.

FORD, E. B., 1955. *Moths*. New Naturalist Series, Collins, London.

FORD, E. B., 1965. *Mendelism and Evolution* (8th edition). Chapman and Hall, London

FROHAWK, F. W., 1924. *Natural History of British Butterflies*, 2 vols. Hutchinson, London.

FROHAWK, F. W., 1938. *Varieties of British Butterflies*. Ward, Lock, London.

GOODSON, A. L. & READ, D. K. [unpublished]. *Aberrational and Subspecific Forms of British Lepidoptera*. British Museum (Natural History). For Internal Use Only.

HARMER A. S., 1987. Breeding the clouded yellow butterfly in 1986. *Entomologist's Rec. J. Var.*, **99**: 227

HARMER, A. S., 1992. [Report of exhibit at Annual Exhibition 1991 - *Colias alfacariensis* Berger breeding on Portland, Dorset]. *Br. J. Ent. Nat. Hist.*, **5**: 50, 51-52.

HARMER, A. S., 1999. A new aberration of the clouded yellow *Colias croceus* (Geoffroy) [ab. *russwurmi*] (Lepidoptera: Pieridae). *Br. J. Ent. Nat. Hist.*, **12**: 93-95, col. pl.

HESLOP, I. R. P., HYDE, G. E., STOCKLEY, R. E., 1964. *Notes & Views of the Purple Emperor*. The Southern Publishing Co., Brighton. **[Illustrated by A. D. A. Russwurm]**

HOVANITZ, W., 1948. Differences in the field activity of two female color phases of *Colias* butterflies at various times of the day. *Contr. Lab. Vert. Biol. Univ. Mich.*, **41**: 1-37.

HOWARTH, T. G., 1973a. *South's British Butterflies*. Frederick Warne, London. **[Illustrated by A. D. A. Russwurm]**

HOWARTH, T. G., 1973b. *Colour Identification Guide to Butterflies of the British Isles*. Frederick Warne, London. **[Illustrated by A. D. A. Russwurm]**

HOWARTH, T. G., 1984. *Colour Identification Guide to Butterflies of the British Isles*, (revised edition) Viking, Harmondsworth. **[Illustrated by A. D. A. Russwurm]**

JARVIS, F. V. L., 1958. Experimental Variation in *Aricia agestis* (Schiff.). *Proc. S. Lond. ent. nat. Hist. Soc.*, **1958**: 94-103, pls VIII, IX.

JONES, A. M., 1992. [Report of exhibit at the Annual Exhibition 1991 - results of breeding *Boloria selene* with central markings of the upperside reduced; *Pararge aegeria* L. ab. *parviocellata* Lempke; and *Lysandra coridon* similar to ab. *cinnameus* B. & L.]. *Br. J. Ent. Nat. Hist.*, **5**: 52.

JONES, A. M., 1996. [Report of exhibit at the Annual Exhibition 1995 - results of breeding *Aricia agestis* ([D. & S.]) ab. *pallidior* Oberthür, and *Strymondia w-album* L., with the hindwing orange band replaced with yellow]. *Br. J. Ent. Nat. Hist.*, **9**: 208.

JONES, R. N. &. KARP. A., 1986. *Introducing Genetics.* John Murray, London.

LEEDS, H. A., 1941. *A Monograph of the British Aberrations of the Chalk-hill Blue Butterfly Lysandra coridon (Poda, 1761).* Addenda. British Aberrations of the Small Copper Butterfly *Lycaena* (*Rumicia*) *phlaeas.* (*Linnaeus* 1761), p. 144. Richmond Hill Printing Works, Bournemouth.

LIPSCOMB, MAJOR-GENERAL C. G., 1978. The Silver-washed Fritillary (*Argynnis paphia* L.): A Population Explosion. *Entomologist's Rec. J. Var.*, **90**: 1-3.

MAJERUS, M. E. N., 1994. *Ladybirds.* The New Naturalist Series, Harper Collins, London.

MAJERUS, M. E. N., 1998. *Melanism: evolution in action.* Oxford University Press, Oxford.

MARCON, REV. J. N., 1980b. *Argynnis paphia* L. and *Limenitis camilla* L. in the New Forest in 1941/42. *Entomologist's Rec. J. Var.*, **92**: 277-279.

MORRISON, P., 1989. *Observers Butterflies.* Frederick Warne, London.
[Illustrated by A. D. A. Russwurm]

PAYNE, J., 1981. Notes on Breeding *Leptidea sinapis* ab. *brunneomaculata* Stauder: the Wood White. *Entomologist's Rec. J. Var.*, **93**: 11-12.

POTTER, N. B. & YOUNG, L. D., 1965. [Report of exhibit at Annual Exhibition 1964 - aberrations of *Lycaena phlaeas* L.]. *Proc. S. Lond. ent. nat. Hist. Soc.*, **1964**: 17.

REVELS, R., 1975a. Notes on Breeding Aberrations of the Chalk Hill Blue: *Lysandra coridon* (Poda). *Entomologist's Rec. J. Var.*, **87**: 281-283, pl. XII.

REVELS, R., 1975b. Notes on Breeding the Ringlet: *Aphantopus hyperantus* (Linn.) ab. *pallens* Schultz and ab. *lanceolata* Shipp. *Entomologist's Rec. J. Var.*, **87**: 283-285, pl. XII.

REVELS, R., 1977a. Notes on breeding ab. *excessa* Tutt of the Gatekeeper (*Pyronia tithonus* L.). *Entomologist's Rec. J. Var.*, **89**: 43-44, pl. VII.

REVELS, R., 1978. Notes on Breeding the Grayling (*Hipparchia semele* L.) ab. *holonops* Brouwer. *Entomologist's Rec. J. Var.*, **90**: 159-161, pl. VIII.

REVELS, R., 1980. Notes on Breeding the Marbled White Butterfly *Melanargia galathea* L. ab *craskei* Tubbs. *Entomologist's Rec. J. Var.*, **92**: 57-60, pl. VI.

REVELS, R., 1998a. Variation on a Theme - Butterfly Aberrations. *British Wildlife*, **9**: 371-377, 16 figs.

ROBERTSON, T. S., 1969-70. Homoeosis and Related Phenomena in the Small Copper Butterfly, *Lycaena phlaeas* L. *Proc. Brit. ent. nat. Hist. Soc.*, **2**: 76-102, 45 figs (1969), **3**: col. pl. (1970).

ROBERTSON, T. S., 1977. Homoeosis in the small copper butterfly, *Lycaena phlaeas* L. *Proc. Brit. ent. nat. Hist. Soc.*, **10**: 96-97, pl. XII, fig. 2, 3 figs.

ROBERTSON, T. S., 1995a. A breeding experiment with the small copper butterfly, *Lycaena phlaeas* (L.) (Lepidoptera: Lycaenidae). *Br. J. Ent. Nat. Hist.*, **8**: 97-101, pl. 1, figs 1-12.

ROBERTSON, T. S. & YOUNG, L. D., 1982. The inheritance and development of spot-pattern variation in the Adonis Blue butterfly, *Lysandra bellargus* (Rottemburg) (Lepidoptera: Lycaenidae). *Entomologist's Gaz.*, **33**: 83-95, pl. 3, 7 figs.

ROBERTSON, T. S. & YOUNG, L. D., 1984. Spot-pattern variation in the Common Blue butterfly, *Polyommatus icarus* (Rottemburg). *Entomologist's Gaz.*, **35**: 1-3, pl. 1.

ROBINSON, R., 1971. *Lepidoptera Genetics.* Pergamon Press, Oxford.

RUSSELL, S. G. CASTLE, 1952. The New Forest in the 'Nineties and After. *Entomologist's Rec. J. Var.*, **64**: 138-144.

RUSSWURM, A. D. A., 1966. Aberrant Lepidoptera taken in the New Forest, Hants., during 1965. *Proc. S. Lond. ent. nat. Hist. Soc.*, **1966**: 61, pl. VI.

RUSSWURM, A. D. A., 1970. A Gynandromorph *Erebia aethiops* Esp. *Entomologist's Rec. J. Var.*, **82**: 252, pl. XV, figs 2, 3.

RUSSWURM, A. D. A., 1971. *Erebia aethiops* Esp. ab. *infasciata* Warren (Lep. Satyridae). *Entomologist's Rec. J. Var.*, **83**: 333, pl. XII. **[Illustrated by A. D. A. Russwurm]**

RUSSWURM, A. D. A., 1976a. Variation in *Lysandra coridon* Poda (Lep.: Lycaenidae), Summer 1975. *Entomologist's Rec. J. Var.*, **88**: 81, pl. IV.

RUSSWURM, A. D. A., 1976b. Aberrations of *Lysandra coridon* Poda (Lep., Lycaenidae) and Other Species, Summer 1976. *Entomologist's Rec. J. Var.*, **88**: 305-306, pl. IX.

RUSSWURM, A. D. A., 1978. *Aberrations of British Butterflies*. E. W. Classey Ltd., Faringdon. **[Illustrated by A. D. A. Russwurm]**

RUSSWURM, A. D. A., 1984. [Report of exhibit at Annual Exhibition 1983 - *Colias croceus* ab. *striata* Geest]. *Proc. Trans. Br. ent. nat. Hist. Soc.*, **17**: 4, pl. 2.

SIBATANI, A., 1983. A Compilation of Data on Wing Homoeosis in Lepidoptera. *J. Res. Lepid.*, **22**: 1-46, 18 figs. Supplement 1, **22**: 118-125, 6 figs.

SKELTON, M., 1999. Successful Overwintering by Clouded Yellow *Colias croceus* (Geoff.) in Southern England. *Atropos*, **8**: 3-6, pls 1, 2.

SOUTH, R., 1906. *The Butterflies of the British Isles*. Frederick Warne, London.

STANDFUSS, M., 1900-01. Synopsis of experiments in hybridization and temperature made with Lepidoptera up to the end of 1898. *Entomologist*, **33**: 161-167; 283-292; 340-348, **34**:11-13, 75-84.

THOMSON, G., 1973. Temperature Effects on *Maniola jurtina* (L.) (Lep. Satyridae). *Entomologist's Rec. J. Var.*, **85**: 109-114, pl. VII.

TUBBS, R., 1978a. [Presidential address: 26th January 1978]. The breeding of butterflies, with special reference to the genetics of aberrational forms. *Proc. Trans. Br. ent. nat. Hist. Soc.*, **11**: 77-87, pls VI, VII, 2 figs.

TUBBS, R., 1978b. A new aberration of *Melanargia galathea* (L.) (Lep.: Satyridae) [ab. *craskei*] from Sussex. *Proc. Trans. Br. ent. nat. Hist. Soc.*, **11**: 87-88, pls VI, VII.

WATSON, R. W., 1967a. New Aberrations of *Callimorpha jacobaeae* Linn. (Lep. Arcti[i]dae). *Entomologist's Rec. J. Var.*, **79**: 33-35, pl. II. **[Illustrated by A. D. A. Russwurm]**

WATSON, R. W., 1967b. [Report of exhibit at the Annual Exhibition 1966 - new aberrations of *Callimorpha jacobaeae* L.]. *Proc. S. Lond. ent. nat. Hist. Soc.*, **1967**: 72, pl. III. **[Illustrated by A. D. A. Russwurm]**

WATSON, R. W., 1968. New Aberrations of *Callimorpha jacobaeae* Linn. (Lep. Arcti[i]dae). *Entomologist's Rec. J. Var.*, **80**: 181-183, pls IX, X. **[Illustrated by A. D. A. Russwurm]**

WATSON, R. W., 1969. [Report of exhibit at the Annual Exhibition 1968 - new aberrations of *Callimorpha jacobaeae* L.]. *Proc. Brit. ent. nat. Hist. Soc.*, **2**: 37, pls V, Va. **[Illustrated by A. D. A. Russwurm]**

WATSON, R. W., 1972a. Further Aberrations of *Callimorpha jacobaeae* Linn. (Lep. Arctiidae). *Entomologist's Rec. J. Var.*, **84**: 11-12, pls I, II. **[Illustrated by A. D. A. Russwurm]**

WATSON, R. W., 1972b. [Aberrations of *Callimorpha jacobaeae* L. shown at Annual Exhibition 1970]. *Proc. Brit. ent. nat. Hist. Soc.*, **4** (4), pls V, VI. **[Illustrated by A. D. A. Russwurm]**

WATSON, R. W., 1975a. Aberrations of *Diacrisia sannio* Hübner (Lep.: Arctiidae). *Entomologist's Rec. J. Var.*, **87**: 258, pl. X. **[Illustrated by A. D. A. Russwurm]**

WATSON, R. W., 1975b. New Aberrations of *Tyria jacobaeae* L. (Lep.: Arctiidae). *Entomologist's Rec. J. Var.*, **87**: 267, pl. XI. **[Illustrated by A. D. A. Russwurm]**

WINOKUR, L., 1995. Understanding size and pattern variation in mainland Britain *Pararge aegeria* L. (Lepidoptera: Satyridae). *Br. J. Ent. Nat. Hist.*, **8**: 102-112, pl. 1, figs 13-21.

FURTHER READING

The following books and papers either contain information on genetics with special reference to inherited variation in butterflies, or are included for their general interest.

ALLAN, R. & GREENWOOD, T., 1999. *Advanced Biology I 1999 Student Resource and Activity Manual.* BIOZONE Learning Media, Glasgow.

ANON., 1952. The Collecting of Aberrations. *Entomologist's Rec. J. Var.,* **64**: 137-138.

BAILEY, K. E. J., 1984. Light and temperature experiments on the Comma butterfly *Polygonia c-album* (Lep.: Nymphalidae). *Proc. Trans. Br. ent. nat. Hist. Soc.,* **17**: 63-65.

BAILEY, K. E. J., 1999. [Report of exhibit at the Annual Exhibition 1998 - results of temperature experiments on larvae and freshly formed pupae of the Nymphalidae]. *Br. J. Ent. Nat. Hist.,* **12**: 142.

BARRINGTON, R. D. G., 1987. Further notes on variation in a north Dorset colony of the meadow brown butterfly, *Maniola jurtina* L. *Entomologist's Rec. J. Var.,* **99**: 97-102, 9 figs.

BARRINGTON, R. D. G., 1988. Extreme unnamed aberrations of *Maniola jurtina* L. (Lep.: Satyridae). *Entomologist's Rec. J. Var.,* **100**: 105-108, 8 figs.

BARRINGTON, R. D. G., 1991a. Continued notes on a North Dorset colony of the Meadow Brown butterfly, *Maniola jurtina* L. *Entomologist's Rec. J. Var.,* **103**: 7-15, 9 figs.

BARRINGTON, R. D. G., 1991b. Additional notes on melanic specimens of the Silver-washed Fritillary (*Argynnis paphia* L.) in North Dorset. *Entomologist's Rec. J. Var.,* **103**: 181-184, 2 figs.

BARRINGTON, R. D. G., 1992b. Breeding *Aphantopus hyperantus* L. ab. *cuneata* Gillmer. *Entomologist's Rec. J. Var.,* **104**: 186-187, 4 figs.

BARRINGTON, R. D. G., 1992c. Additional notes on aberrations of the Meadow Brown (*Maniola jurtina* L.) from North Dorset. *Entomologist's Rec. J. Var.,* **104**: 315-319, 11 figs.

BARRINGTON, R. D. G., 1994b. Breeding *Eurodryas aurinia* Rott. Ab. *virgata* Tutt. *Br. J. Ent. Nat. Hist.,* **7**: 97-98, 1 fig.

BARRINGTON, R. D. G., 1995. A breeding experiment with *Para[r]ge aegeria* L. ab. *schmidti* Dioz. (Lep.: Satyridae). *Entomologist's Rec. J. Var.,* **107**: 179-180, 4 figs.

BARRINGTON, R. D. G., 1996. [Report of exhibit at the Annual Exhibition 1995 - homoeosis in *Pieris napi* L.]. *Br. J. Ent. Nat. Hist.,* **9**: 207.

BARRINGTON, R. D. G., 1999b. The influence of childhood on an entomologist and a very rare fritillary. *Entomologist's Rec. J. Var.,* **111**: 261-265, pl. A.

BERRY, R. J., 1977. *Inheritance and Natural History.* New Naturalist Series, Collins, London.

BROWN, A. D. R., 1970. A New Aberration of *Erynnis tages* L. [ab. *radiata*] (Lep.: Hesperiidae). *Entomologist's Rec. J. Var.,* **82**: 253, pl. XV, fig. 1.

CALLOW, M., 1993. [Report of exhibit at the Annual Exhibition 1992 - results of breeding from *Aricia agestis* ([D & S]) female with enlarged and outwardly displaced spotting]. *Br. J. Ent. Nat. Hist.,* **6**: 50, pl. II, fig. 3.

CALLOW, M., 1995. [Report of exhibit at the Annual Exhibition 1994 - homoeosis in *Anthocharis cardamines* L.]. *Br. J. Ent. Nat. Hist.,* **8**: 178.

CALLOW, M., 1998a. [Report of exhibit at the Annual Exhibition 1996 - a possibly unique *Aphantopus hyperantus* L. bilateral gynandromorph: typical male left side and ab. *arete* Müller female left side]. *Br. J. Ent. Nat. Hist.,* **10**: 146, pl. 1, fig. 7.

CALLOW, M., 1998b. [Report of exhibit at the Annual Exhibition 1997 - unexpected appearance of *Aphantopus hyperantus* L. ab. *pallens* Schultz in F_4 generation from ab. *arete* Müller female]. *Br. J. Ent. Nat. Hist.,* **11**: 82, pl. V, fig. 2.

CHATFIELD, J., 1987. *F. W. Frohawk: his life and work.* The Crowood Press, Marlborough.

COCKAYNE, E. A., 1916. *Agriades coridon* var. *roystonensis*. *Entomologist's Rec. J. Var.*, **28**: 58-59.

COCKAYNE, E. A., 1921. Structural abnormalities in the Lepidoptera. *Trans. Lond. nat. Hist. Soc.*, 10-69, pl. 1.

COCKAYNE, E. A., 1930. Insect teratology. *Trans. R. ent. Soc., Lond.*, **82**: 209-226, pls 11-13.

COCKAYNE, E. A., 1951. A note on the genetics of *Colias croceus* Fourcroy ab. *cinerascens* Rowland Brown. *Entomologist's Rec. J. Var.*, **63**: 199-200.

COCKAYNE, E. A., 1952a. Aberrations of *Lysandra coridon* Poda and *L. bellargus* Rott. What are the causation factors? *Entomologist's Rec. J. Var.*, **64**: 157-160, pls VI, VII.

COCKAYNE, E. A., 1952b. *Colias croceus* Fourcroy ab. *duplex* Cockerell. The story of a fraud. *Entomologist's Rec. J. Var.*, **64**: 193-194.

COLLIER, MAJOR A. E., 1956a. A Successful Rearing of *Aphantopus hyperantus* Linn. ab. *lanceolata* Shipp. *Entomologist's Rec. J. Var.*, **68** 1-2.

COLLIER, MAJOR A. E., 1959a. Some Light on the Genetics of *Pyrgus malvae* L. ab. *taras* Bergstr. *Entomologist's Rec. J. Var.*, **71**: 203.

COLLIER, MAJOR A. E., 1967a. A New Aberration of *Aphantopus hyperantus* [ab. *chrysophalaros*] (Lep.: Satyridae). *Entomologist's Rec. J. Var.*, **79**: 4, pl.1.

COLLIER, MAJOR A. E., 1967b. The Genetics of *Lysandra coridon* Poda ab. *semi syngrapha* Tutt. *Entomologist's Rec. J. Var.*, **79**: 4.

CRIBB, P., 1983. *Breeding the British Butterflies*. Amateur Entomologists' Society, Hanworth.

DAVIES, D. A. L., 1957. Variation in *Colias croceus* (Fourc.) ab. *helice* Hb. *Entomologist's Rec. J. Var.*, **69**: 205-206.

DENNIS, R. C., 1994. [Report of exhibit at the Annual Exhibition 1993 - results of a breeding experiment with *Pyronia tithonus* L. transitional to ab. *caeca* Tutt]. *Br. J. Ent. Nat. Hist.*, **7**: 146.

DENNIS, R. C., 1995. [Report of exhibit at the Annual Exhibition 1994 - results of a breeding experiment with *Pyronia tithonus* L. ab. *caeca* Tutt]. *Br. J. Ent. Nat. Hist.*, **8**: 178, pl. II, fig.3.

DE WORMS, BARON, 1962. *The Macrolepidoptera of Wiltshire*. The Wiltshire Archaeological and Natural History Society.

DICKSON, R., 1976. *A Lepidopterist's Handbook*. Amateur Entomologists' Society, Hanworth.

DYSON, R. C., 1952. Notes on breeding *Polyommatus icarus* Rott. and Foodplants for Blues. *Entomologist's Rec. J. Var.*, **64**: 194-195.

ELLIS, H. A., 1995. An example of extreme f. *pan-albisignata* Kaaber & Høegh-Guldberg, in the Durham Argus butterfly, *Aricia artaxerxes salmacis*, Stephens, and related observations. *Entomologist's Rec. J. Var.*, **107**: 133-141, pl. C, figs 3, 4.

FORD, E. B., 1975. *Ecological Genetics*, (4th edition). Chapman and Hall, London.

FORD, R. L. E., 1952. Varieties of the Holly Blue, *Lycaenopsis argiolus* L., with five figures. *Entomologist's Gaz.*, **3**: 52-55, 5 figs.

FRIEDRICH, E., 1986. *Breeding Butterflies and Moths - A practical Handbook for British and European Species*. Harley Books, Colchester.

FROHAWK, F. W., 1934. *The Complete Book of British Butterflies*. Ward, Lock, London.

GAINSFORD, CAPT. A. P., 1970. An Extreme Aberration of *Lycaena phlaeas* L. [ab. *berviniensis* Smith]. *Entomologist's Rec. J. Var.*, **82**: 202, 2 figs.

GAINSFORD, CAPT. A. P., 1975. *Mellicta athalia* Rottemburg in East Cornwall, 1974. *Entomologist's Rec. J. Var.*, **87**: 172-175.

GARDINER, B. O. C., 1962. An albino form of *Pieris brassicae* Linnaeus (Lep., Pieridae). *Entomologist's Gaz.*, **13**: 97-100, pl. 1.

GARDINER, B. O. C., 1963. Genetic and environmental variation in *Pieris brassicae*. *Journ. Res. Lep.*, Vol. 2. No 2: 127-136.

GARDINER, B. O. C., 1974. An unusual aberration of *Pieris brassicae* (Linnaeus) (Lep., Pieridae). *Entomologist's Gaz.*, **25**: 186, pl. 11.

GARDINER, B. O. C., 1979. A review of variation in *Pieris brassicae* (L.) (Lep., Pieridae). *Proc. Trans. Br. Ent. nat. Hist. Soc.*, **12**: 24-46, pls III-VI, 2 text figs.

GOODSON, A. L., 1951. The colour forms of *Colias croceus* ab. *helice* Hübner. *Entomologist's Rec. J. Var.*, **63**: 47.

GOODSON, A. L., 1966. Aberrations of British Macrolepidoptera. *Entomologist's Rec. J. Var.* **78**: 151-153, pl. VI.

HØEGH-GULDBERG, O., 1974. Natural Pattern Variation and the Effect of Cold Treatment in the Genus *Aricia* R. L. (Lepidoptera, Lycaenidae). (Aricia Study No. 14). *Proc. Brit. ent. nat. Hist. Soc.*, **7**: 37-44, pls III, IV.

HOPE, M. A., 1988. A rare spotless aberration of the Gatekeeper. *Bull. amat. Ent. Soc.*, **47**: 217-220, 2 figs.

HOWARTH, T. G., 1971a. Descriptions of a new British Subspecies of *Pararge aegeria* (L.) and an Aberration of *Cupido minimus* (Fuessly) (Lep., Lycaenidae) [ab. *multistriata*]. *Entomologist's Gaz.*, **22**: 117-118.

HOWARTH, T. G., 1971b. The Status of Irish *Hipparchia semele* (L.) (Lep., Satyridae) with Descriptions of a new Subspecies and Aberrations. *Entomologist's Gaz.*, **22**: 123-129, pl.1.

HUXLEY, J. & CARTER, D. J., 1981. A blue form of the Small Skipper, *Thymelicus flavus* (Bruennich) (Lepidoptera: Hesperiidae), with comments on colour production. *Entomologist's Gaz.*, **32**: 79-82, pls 4, 5.

JARVIS, F. V. L., 1955. Lethality in *Colias croceus* (Fourcroy). *Entomologist's Rec. J. Var.*, **67**: 137-139.

JONES, A. M., 1989. [Report of exhibit at the Annual Exhibition 1988 - results of breeding *Pararge aegeria* L. ab. *antico-excessa* Lempke]. *Br. J. Ent. Nat. Hist.*, **2**: 31.

JONES, A. M., 1990. [Report of exhibit at the Annual Exhibition 1989 - results of breeding *Pararge aegeria* L. ab. *parviocellata* Lempke and a new aberration with pale markings coalesced between veins 2 & 3, and 3 & 4; *Lycaena phlaeas* L. ab. *radiata* Tutt]. *Br. J. Ent. Nat. Hist.*, **3**: 63-64, pl. III, figs 1, 2.

JONES, A. M., 1991. [Report of exhibit at the Annual Exhibition 1990 - results of breeding *Lycaena phlaeas* L. ab. *schmidtii* Gerhardt; *Pararge aegeria* L., with pale markings coalesced between veins 2 & 3 and 3 & 4]. *Br. J. Ent. Nat. Hist.*, **4**: 21.

JONES, G. & JONES, M., 1984. *Biology GCSE edition*. Cambridge University Press, Cambridge.

KETTLEWELL, B., 1973. *The Evolution of Melanism*. Clarendon Press, Oxford.

LEEDS, H. A., 1948. British Aberrations of the Gatekeeper Butterfly, *Maniola tithonus* (Linnaeus 1771); Meadow Brown Butterfly, *Maniola jurtina* (Linnaeus 1758); and the Small Heath Butterfly, *Coenonympha pamphilus* (Linnaeus 1758). *Proc. Trans. S. Lond. ent. nat. Hist. Soc.*, **1948-49**: 80-122b, pls V-VII.

LEEDS, H. A., 1951. Postscript by H. A. Leeds to his paper on the British Aberrations of the Gatekeeper Butterfly, *Maniola tithonus* (Lin.); Meadow Brown Butterfly, *Maniola jurtina* (Lin.); and the Small Heath Butterfly, *Coenonympha pamphilus* (Lin.). *Proc. Trans. S. Lond. ent. nat. Hist. Soc.*, **1949-1950**: 81-82.

LEMPKE, B. J., 1956. On Some Forms of *Aglais urticae* L. *Entomologist's Rec. J. Var.*, **68**: 282-285.

LIPSCOMB, MAJOR-GENERAL C. G., 1959. Variations of *Aglais urticae* L. *Entomologist's Rec. J. Var.*, **71**: 146-149.

LIPSCOMB, MAJOR-GENERAL C. G., 1966. *Lysandra bellargus* Rott., A New Aberration [ab. *totonigra*]. *Entomologist's Rec. J. Var.*, **78**: 78.

LIPSCOMB, MAJOR-GENERAL C. G., 1967. Variation in *Aphantopus hyperanthus* Linn. *Entomologist's Rec. J. Var.*, **79**: 127-129.

LIPSCOMB, MAJOR-GENERAL C. G., 1968. Breeding *Lysandra coridon* ab. *syngrapha*. *Entomologist's Rec. J. Var.*, **80**: 284-285.

LIPSCOMB, MAJOR-GENERAL C. G., 1979. Heat Aberrations of *Aglais urticae* L. *Entomologist's Rec. J. Var.*, **91**: 326-327.

LIPSCOMB, MAJOR-GENERAL C. G., 1980. A New Form of *Maniola jurtina* L. related to *M. jurtina* ab. *postaurolancia* [*sic*] Leeds. *Entomologist's Rec. J. Var.*, **92**: 205, pl. XVIII.

MARCON, REV. J. N., 1975. Reminiscences of a Butterfly Hunter. *Entomologist's Rec. J. Var.*, **87**: 7-10.

MARCON, REV. J. N., 1976. The Hazards of the Chase. *Entomologist's Rec. J. Var.*, **88**: 213-217.

MARCON, REV. J. N., 1978. Further memoirs of a Butterfly Hunter. *Entomologist's Rec. J. Var.*, **90**: 167-169.

MARCON, REV. J. N., 1980a. Further Reminiscences of a Butterfly Hunter. *Entomologist's Rec. J. Var.*, **92**: 34-37.

MCLEOD, L., 1968. A New Aberration of *Pieris brassicae* (Linn.) [ab. *marginavenata*] Lepidoptera, Pieridae. *Entomologist's Rec. J. Var.*, **80**: 127-129, pl. VII.

MILES, P. M., 1976. Absence of discal spots in the Small White butterfly *Pieris rapae* (Linnaeus) (Lep., Pieridae). *Entomologist's Gaz.*, **27**: 33-34, pl. 3.

NEWMAN, E., 1871-72. *An Illustrated Natural History of British Butterflies and Moths.* William Glaisher, London.

NIJHOUT, H. FREDERICK., 1991. *Development and Evolution of Butterfly Wing Patterns.* Smithsonian Instn. P.

OATES, M., 1996. The Demise of Butterflies in the New Forest. *British Wildlife*, **7**: 205-216.

PARSONS, M. & HADLEY, M., 1987. Abbot's Wood - A history of a woodland and its butterflies. *Entomologist's Rec. J. Var.*, **99**: 49-58, 1 fig., 1 table.

PICKETT, C. P., 1916. *Agriades coridon* var. *roystonensis* from the Herts District, 1915. *Entomologist's Rec. J. Var.*, **28**: 59-62.

PILLEAU, N. C., 1954. A Rare Aberration of *Aphantopus hyperantus* Linn. [ab. *caeca* Fuchs]. *Entomologist's Rec. J. Var.*, **66**: 242-243.

PITMAN, C. M. R., 1960. Controlled Temperature Experiments with *Vanessa atalanta* L., *V. cardui* L. and *Aglais urticae* L. *Entomologist's Rec. J. Var.*, **72**: 1-8.

PORTER, J., 1997. *The Colour Identification Guide to Caterpillars of the British Isles.* Viking, London.

REVELS, R., 1977b. Further Notes on Breeding *Lysandra coridon* (Poda) ab. *fowleri* South. *Entomologist's Rec. J. Var.*, **89**: 45-46, pl. VIII.

REVELS, R., 1998b. [Report of exhibit at the Annual Exhibition 1997 - results of breeding experiment with *Aricia agestis* ([D. & S.]) ab. *glomerata* Tutt]. *Br. J. Ent. Nat. Hist.*, **11**: 83.

ROBERTSON, T. S., 1980. Weather and variation in *Argynnis paphia* (Linnaeus) (Lepidoptera: Nymphalidae). *Entomologist's Gaz.*, **31**: 93-102, 2 figs.

ROBERTSON, T. S., 1985. A short-tailed aberration of the Swallowtail Butterfly, *Papilio machaon* Linnaeus (Lepidoptera: Papilionidae). *Entomologist's Gaz.*, **36**: 183-185, pl. 8.

ROBERTSON, T. S., 1995b. Geographical variation in the blue (interference) coloration of *Polyommatus icarus* (Rottemburg) (Lepidoptera: Lycaenidae) in the British Isles. *Entomologist's Gaz.*, **46**: 183-187.

ROBERTSON, T. S. & YOUNG, L. D., 1987. Spot-pattern variation in *Polyommatus icarus* (Rottemburg) (Lepidoptera: Lycaenidae): further breeding experiments. *Entomologist's Gaz.*, **38**: 1-10, pl. 1, 8 figs.

SHEPHERD, J., 1942. Breeding Experiments with the Irish Yellow Race of *Pieris napi*. *Entomologist*, **75**: 233-235.

SHEPPARD, P. M., 1958. *Natural Selection and Heredity.* Hutchinson, London.

SIVITER SMITH, P., 1952. The White and Pale Forms of *Lycaena phlaeas* L. *Entomologist's Rec. J. Var.*, **64**: 134-136.

SYMES, H., 1956. Hell Coppice in the 1930's. *Entomologist's Rec. J. Var.*, **68**: 98-102.

THOMAS, J. & LEWINGTON, R., 1991. *The Butterflies of Britain and Ireland*. Dorling Kindersley, London.

THOMSON, G., 1970. New Forms of *Maniola jurtina* L. (Lep. Satyridae). *Entomologist's Rec. J. Var.*, **82**: 189-192, pl. X.

TOOLE, G. & TOOLE, S., 1995. *Understanding Biology for Advanced Level* (3rd edition). Stanley Thornes, Cheltenham.

TUBBS, C. R., 1986. *The New Forest*. New Naturalist Series, William Collins Son's, London.

TUTT, J. W., 1896. *British Butterflies*. Hedgerow & Woodland Series, George Gill & Sons, London.

TUTT, J. W., 1905-1914. *A Natural History of the British Butterflies*, 4 vols, Elliot Stock, London.

TUTT, J. W., 1994. *Practical Hints for the Field Lepidopterist*. A Facsimile Reprint. Amateur Entomologists' Society, Orpington.

WARRIER, R. EVERETT, 1951. On breeding *Colias croceus* Fourcroy [ab. *cinerascens* Rowland Brown]. *Entomologist's Rec. J. Var.*, **63**: 198-199, pl. VI.

WILLIAMS, H. B., 1951. A new aberration of *Melanargia galathea* L. [ab. *valentini*]. *Entomologist's Gaz.*, **2**: 247-248, pl. 7.

WILLIAMS, H. B., 1957. The Variation of Euchloë cardamines L. *Proc. S. Lond. ent. nat. Hist. Soc.*, **1957**: 82-88, pl. V.

WINOKUR, L., 1996. Wing homoeosis in *Pararge aegeria* L. (Lepidoptera: Satyridae). *Br. J. Ent. Nat. Hist.*, **9**: 193-195, 1 fig.

SOCIETIES AND OTHER
SOURCES OF INFORMATION

Over the years many aberrant butterflies have been exhibited at the Annual Exhibition of the British Entomological and Natural History Society and this continues to be the case. Some of these specimens have been illustrated in the Society's Proceedings and Transactions which are currently incorporated in the *British Journal of Entomology and Natural History*.

Details of the Society may be obtained from the Secretary, Dinton Pastures Country Park, Davis Street, Hurst, Reading, Berkshire RG10 0TH, or from the Society's website at http://www.bens.org.uk

Back numbers of the Society's publications are obtainable from the Sales Secretary at the same address.

From time to time relevant articles on aberration in butterflies appear in the following publications:

Atropos. Available from 36 Tinker Lane, Meltham, Huddersfield, West Yorkshire HD7 3EX. E-mail: atropos@atroposed.freeserve.co.uk

Entomologist's Gazette. Available from Gem Publishing Co., Brightwood, Brightwell, Wallingford, Oxon OX10 0QD.

The Bulletin of the Amateur Entomologists' Society. The A.E.S., P. O. Box 8774, London SW7 5ZG. http://www.theaes.org

The Entomologist's Record and Journal of Variation. Available from the Register, R. F. McCormick, F. R. E. S. 36 Paradise Rd., Teignmouth, Devon TQ14 8NR.

GENERAL INDEX

References to the colour plates and figures are in bold type. References to pages in the text are in Arabic Numerals and those to pages preceding the Introduction are in Roman Numerals. Numerals in italic refer to illustrations in the text. The names of aberrations and forms are listed alphabetically under the specific name.

homoeosis 53, 54, 83-4, *87*, 91 (*see also phlaeas*)
homogametic sex 77, 78
homologous chromosomes (or homologues) 57
homozygote 57
homozygous 57
Honister Pass, Cumberland 22
Hope Collection, Oxford 20
Horseshoe Vetch (*see Hippocrepis*)
Hovanitz, W. 65
Howarth, T. G. 3, 15, 22, *34*, 40, *49*, 53
Hughes, C. N. 3
Humming-bird Hawk-moth (*see stellatarum*)
hyale, Colias 18
hybridization 54, 82
hydrogen cyanide 98
hyperantus, Aphantopus **83-84**, 20, 62, 64, *90*, 95-6
    arete Müller, ab. **84: 4**, *90*, 95
    genetics 64-5, 95-6
    lanceolata Shipp, ab. **83**, 20, 62, *90*, 95
    lanceolata Shipp + *arete* Müller, ab. *90*, 95
    nov., ab. - hindwing ocelli with white pupils
        well-developed **84: 3**
    pallens Schultz, ab. 65
    pathological **84: 1,2**

I

icarus icarus, Polyommatus **19**, **20**, 67, 74, *88*, 91 93
    antico-obsoleta Tutt, ab. **20: 4**
    antico-obsoleta Tutt + *postico-striata* Tutt, ab. **20: 1**
    antico-striata Tutt, ab. **20: 6**
    antico-striata Tutt + *subobsoleta* Tutt, ab. **20: 2**
    apicata-supracaerulea Tutt, ab. **19: 5**
    arcuata Weymer, ab. 67
    basijuncta Tutt, ab. 67
    bilateral gynandromorph 74
    costajuncta Tutt, ab. 67
    elongata Tutt, ab. 67, 74, 91
    extensa Tutt, ab. 91
    genetics 67, 74, 91
    parvipuncta Tutt + *albescens* Tutt
        + *barnumi* Dujardin, ab. **20: 3**
    radiata Courvoisier, ab. *88*, 91
    rufina Oberthür, ab. **19: 8**
    striata Tutt, ab. 93
    transiens Tutt 67, 74
    well-developed lunules **19: 6**
icarus mariscolore, Polyommatus **19**, 82
    gynandromorph, bilateral **19: 1,2**
    gynandromorph, mixed **19: 3,4**
    gynandromorphism 82
    well-developed lunules **19: 7**
inbreeding depression 62
incomplete dominance 67
industrial melanics 65
inheritance 55 *et seq.*
    dihybrid 67-70 (*diag.*), 92, 95
    monohybrid 62-7, 63 (*diag.*), 66 (*diag.*)
    multifactorial (or polygenic) 72-4, 91, 92
    sex 77 (*diag.*), 78
    sex limited (or sex-controlled) 66, 78-9
    sex-linked 62, 79 (*diag.*), 80, 92
intermediate cells 60, 68, 69 (*diag.*)

intersex 82-3 (*see also argus*)
intersexes 54
Intersexes in the Lycaenidae 83
io, Inachis **42**, 22, 26
    belisaria Oberthür, ab. 22
    exoculata Weymer, ab. **42: 2,3**
    fulva Oudemans, ab. **42: 1**
iris, Apatura **33-36**, 1, 37, 95
    iolata Cabeau, ab. **34**
    lugenda Cabeau, ab. **35**; **36: 3**
    sorbioduni Heslop, ab. **36: 1,2**
    typical **33**
Isle of Pemba 10
Isle of Wight 25

J

jacobaeae, Tyria 41, *47*
    coneyi Watson, ab. *47*
    intermedia Watson, ab. *47*
    nigrofimbriata Watson, ab. *47*
    typical *47*
Jarvis, F. V. L. 75
Joint Committee for the Conservation of Insects 97
Jones, A. M. 64
Jones, R. N. & Karp, A. 78, 81
jurtina insularis, Maniola **78-79**, 17, 24, 73, 76, *89*, *90*, 95
    addenda Mousley, ab. 73
    alba Blackie, ab. **78: 3**
    anommata Verity, ab. **79: 1**, *90*, 95
    anticrassipuncta Leeds, ab. 23
    bilateral gynandromorph *89*, 95
    fracta Zweigelt, ab. 74
    genetics 73-4, 76, 95
    nov., ab. **79: 4**
    postmultifidus Lipscomb, ab. **79: 2,3**, 74
    radiata Frohawk, ab. **78: 1,2**
    transformis Leeds, ab. **78: 4**

K

Kimbolton, Huntingdonshire 14, 17
Kings of Lymington 1

L

Lake District, Cumberland 22
Large Blue (*see arion*)
Large Heath (*see tullia*)
Large Skipper (*see venata*)
Large Tortoiseshell (*see polychloros*)
Law of Independent Assortment (Segregation)
    (*see* Mendel)
Law of Segregation (*see* Mendel)
Leeds, H. A. 84
Leighton Buzzard, Bedfordshire 7, 10
Lepidoptera Genetics 82
Life of the Meadow Brown, The 73
Lipscombe, Maj.-Gen. C. G. 2, 75, 96
Lisbon 7, 8